Piano Blues Scales

Major And Minor For Piano

Southern House Publishing

ISBN: 978-1-9196118-5-3

tylermusic.co.uk

CONTENTS

Introduction

Scales are a fundamental aspect of any kind of music and with their knowledge comes a greater understanding and ability. The blues scales are unusual in some respects as according to traditional music theory they aren't actually considered to be true scales, being the pentatonic scales with an additional note, but in reality they are most definitely a real thing, having been used for years within many popular styles of music, blues and boogie-woogie being the most obvious, but certainly not the only styles.

Like all things in life there are degrees of knowledge, and you can know a set of scales, and then you can *really* know a set of scales. It is of course the latter position that you ideally want to find yourself, knowing scales inside out will really help you play or improvise in many styles of music.

In order to help with this, the book shows each scale presented in a clearly and explained along with fingering suggestions. This is followed by various ideas of how to practice the scales in a more reality based musical fashion, in order to help the piano player when playing/improvising.

The main target audience for this book is perhaps the blues and boogie-woogie piano crowd, but as already mentioned, the use of the blues scales expands into many popular styles, so hopefully it will be useful to many more.

How To Use The Book

This book intends to show the various blues-scales in order that they can be learnt and memorised, but it intends to go further than this, with the idea being to help learn how to use the scales or sections of them in ways that will actually help in improvisation. First, learning to play them in their entirety, then in different sections and patterns and ultimately learning how to combine them. Twelve keys are included, with no need to complicate matters with en-harmonic equivalents that have no bearing on the subject.

So how should you approach the book?

It's up to you to an extent, but if we are realistic it might not be practical to learn every scale at once. I mean you can, but it depends on how much time and energy you have for this. Personally, with this in mind, I would choose a few (those keys that you tend to play the most at this time) and start with them. Only once you feel ready to learn others should you do so. This might mean you concentrate on the minor-blues to start with, or you might work on both the major and minor of one specific key, this is personal choice, but it's best to take small steps to begin with.

When learning a scale, I'd begin by practising it over one octave and concentrate on the fingering while you are doing so. Get it right moving up the scale (root note to root note) and then try it moving down, when you are happy you can then practise them up and down. Once you are comfortable with this you can think about playing it over a two octave range and then three octaves. Every-time you add an extra octave it will become a little trickier to keep it going.

Once you feel competent with the simple up and down movement of the scale, you can then move to the second section of the book. This will go over some ideas of practising in different ways, and perhaps in a more musical fashion that will help when actually playing or improvising.

Fingering

To help with learning the scales, included are some fingering suggestions that use the standard numbering system. As such the thumbs are referred to as being number one, with the little fingers being number five. These fingerings are suggestions only, if you feel another way of playing suits you better, then by all means don't feel that you have to follow them blindly to the letter.

Fingering Number Diagram

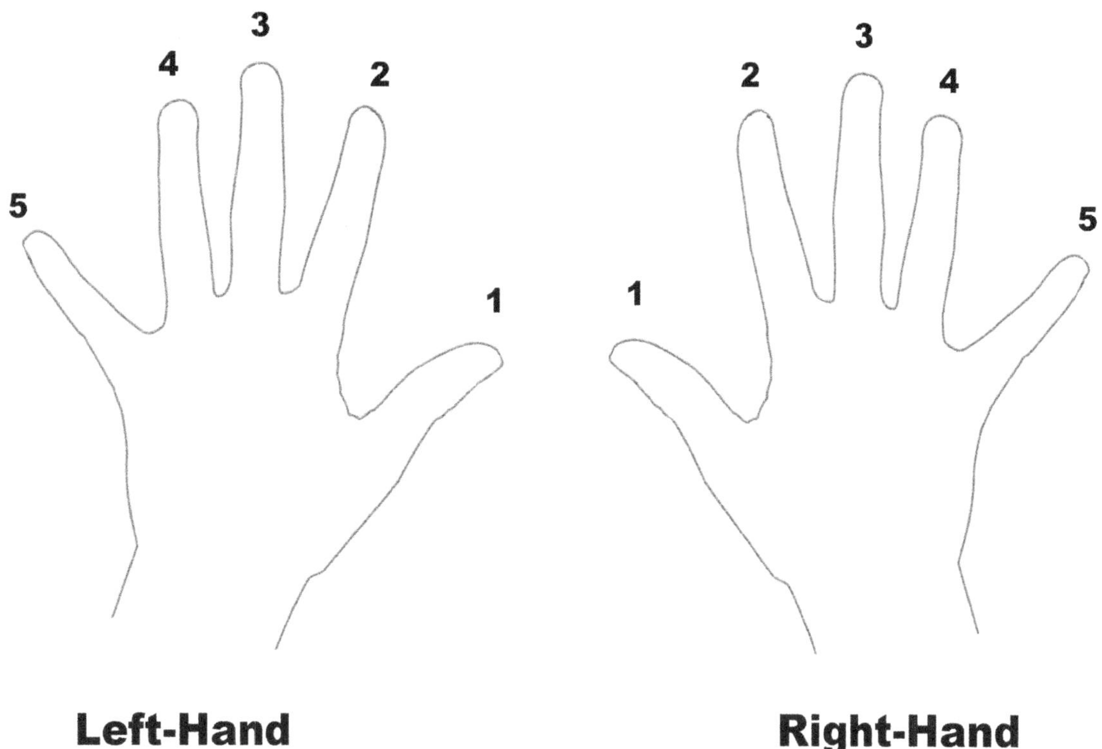

IMPORTANT NOTE

It's important to note that the blues-scales don't really have set fingerings like the normal major or minor scales for example. There is no designated 'correct' way to play these as such, but that said, there are still a few basic ideas/rules that should be known, as they will help you with whatever you are playing.

Scale Starting Points

A good general rule regarding starting a scale is that if it begins on a white key then it's best to use your thumb (Finger no.1). If the scale starts with a black key, then it works better to begin with your index finger (no.2).
This is a general rule for all scales due to how our hands work over the keyboard, that said, there are a few scales that don't quite comply with this, but they are the minority, so as a rule, stick to the rule.

Moving The Thumb Under

Generally you find most scales follow a 1-2-3-1 pattern or similar. As you move through the scale you will run out of fingers and get to a point where you can't continue. Here we have to move the thumb over, slipping under the fingers and onto the next key, so allowing the rest of the fingering to continue on. There's no set formula as to when you do this, but it's often after three notes. One rule is that you ideally want the thumb to land on a white key, so the fingering will need to be ordered as such to work around this. As such, the thumb tends to be used after a black key moving upwards and before one moving downwards, that's not always the case, but it's a good general rule.

Include More Fingers

Remember to try to use as many fingers as possible. While it might be possible to play some scales using only your thumb and first two fingers (1-2-3) or in some cases even less (two fingers) it makes sense to use as many fingers as possible. This makes for a smoother more efficient action, less moving/jumping of the hand, it also gives you more options as you won't find yourself limited in what you can play.

Now having said that, there are times when using only two or three fingers actually works very well, even preferable over using too many fingers that can make a jumble. Watch some top blues (or even jazz) players, and you will see all sorts of fingering combinations going on, which leads me to the next point.

Be Open Minded/Adaptive

As said before, try not to get bogged down in exact rules or absolute correct ways. The blues goes against some standard music theory and this also leads itself into how it is played. Improvisation is supposed to be open and free, creating new ideas on the fly, to do this effectively you need to be open with the fingering. Learn the basic ideas and patterns and then let yourself go and do what feels right and fits that moment in time. It doesn't happen overnight but with continued practice we can all get better.

Blues Scales Basics

Minor-Blues Scale

Perhaps the more commonly known of the two, often being referred to as 'the blues-scale', but of course it's not alone having the major version to keep it company. It's an adaption of the minor pentatonic scale having the addition of the flat-fifth.

It is a six note scale with the seventh note being a repeat of the root, it consists of the root, flat-third, fourth, flat-fifth, fifth and flat-seventh degrees of a major scale.

Degrees Of Major Scale

Intervals Used Moving Through The Scale

Whole&Half	Whole	Half	Half	Whole&Half	Whole

Major-Blues Scale

Slightly less known perhaps, the major-blues scale is no less important than the minor, being common in many styles of music. It's an adaption of the major pentatonic scale with the addition of the flat-third to give that 'blues' spin to it.

It is a six note scale with the seventh note being a repeat of the root, it consists of the root, second, flat-third, third, fifth, and sixth degrees of a major scale.

Degrees Of Major Scale

Intervals Used Moving Through The Scale

Whole	Half	Half	Whole&Half	Whole	Whole&Half

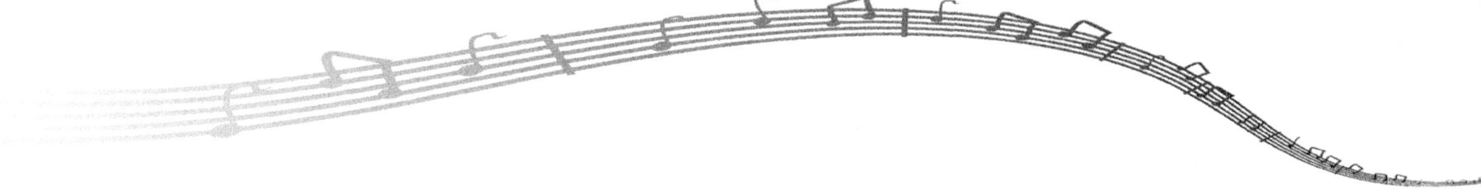

Minor-Blues Scales

A – Minor Blues

The first scale in the book is the 'A' minor-blues scale. This particular scale works nicely over the piano keyboard, with only one black key to contend with your fingers can fall smoothly over the key-bed, making this one of the nicer keys for this particular scale.

Shown As Degrees

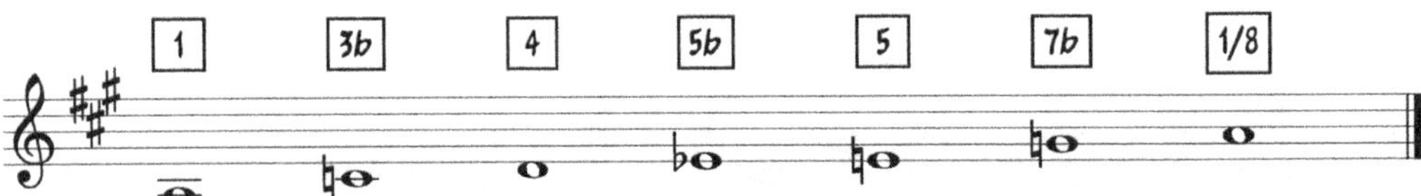

Shown As Named

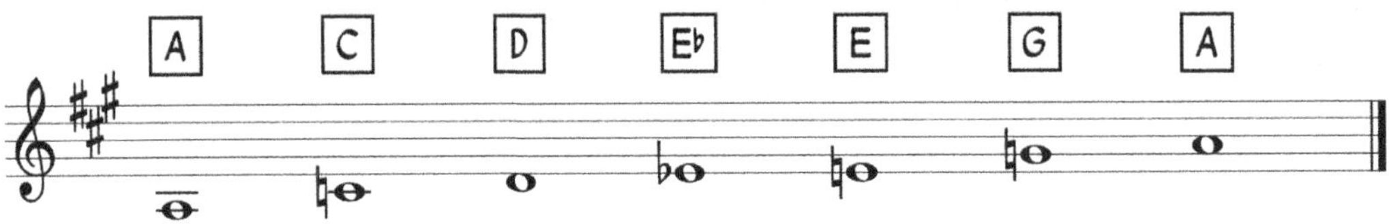

Fingering Suggestion   (Right-Hand)

1.   When not moving any higher.

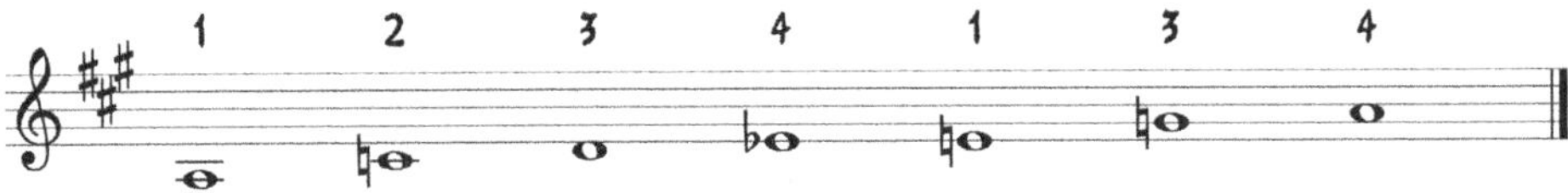

2.   When continuing on further up.

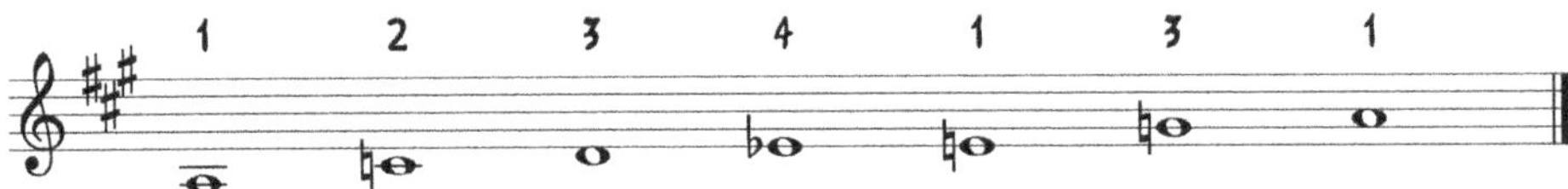

> The thumb (1) is crossed over at the top *if* the scale is to continue on up into another octave, otherwise there is no need for the extra movement and the finger (4) can be used.

B♭ – Minor Blues

The 'B♭' major blues scale uses two black keys so isn't too hard to remember, although it does begin on a black key which always makes the fingering a little more awkward.

Shown As Degrees

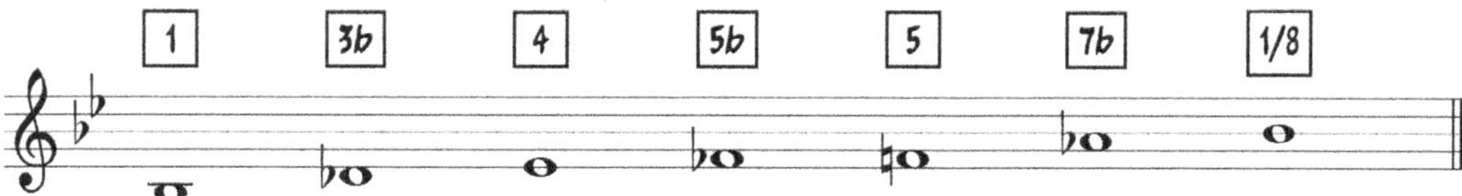

Shown As Named

Fingering Suggestions   (Right-Hand)

1. When not moving any higher.

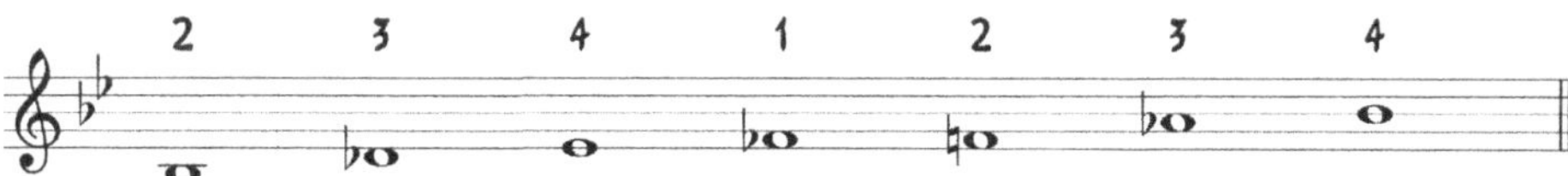

2. When continuing on further up.

There are various ways to approach this one, but I'd stay with the common rule of not starting with the thumb on a black key. If moving up further, in order to get finger (2) back onto the root at the top, it's necessary to use the thumb again on the 'G'.

B – Minor Blues

Although the key of 'B' does have five sharps, because of the make-up of the blues scale it only uses one black key for the 'B' minor blue-scale.

Shown As Degrees

Shown As Named

Fingering Suggestion   (Right-Hand)

1. When not moving any higher.

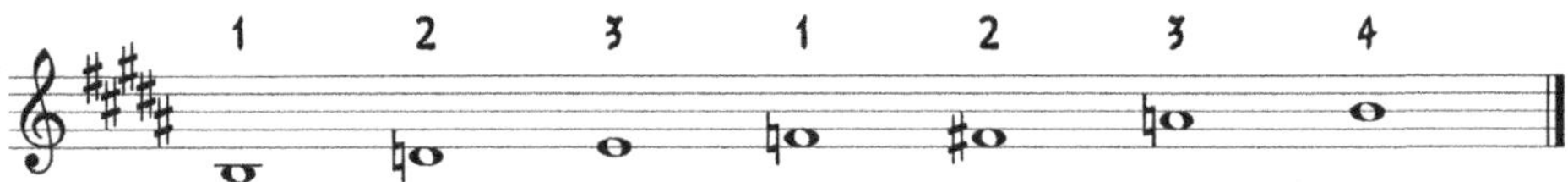

2. When continuing on further up.

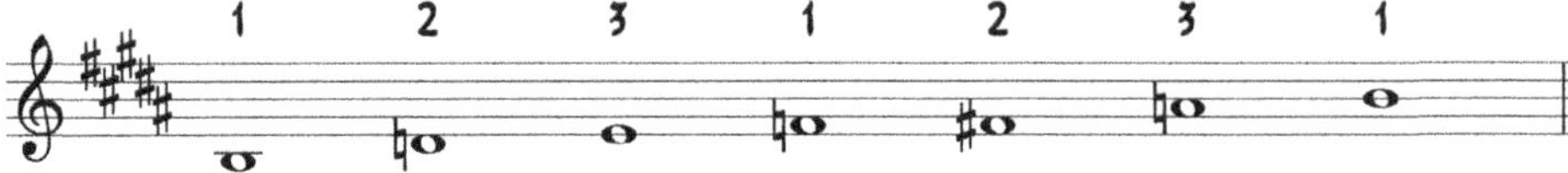

The thumb (1) is crossed over at the top *if* the scale is to continue on up into another octave, otherwise there is no need for the extra movement and finger (4) can be used.

C – Minor Blues

Probably the first version of the blues scale that most people learn on the piano. With only two black notes to contend with this one is not too difficult, although it doesn't fall under the fingers quite as smoothly as some other keys. That may surprise, as the key of 'C' is usually the easiest generally speaking, but of course it's not just white keys anymore, having three black keys to contend with.

Shown As Degrees

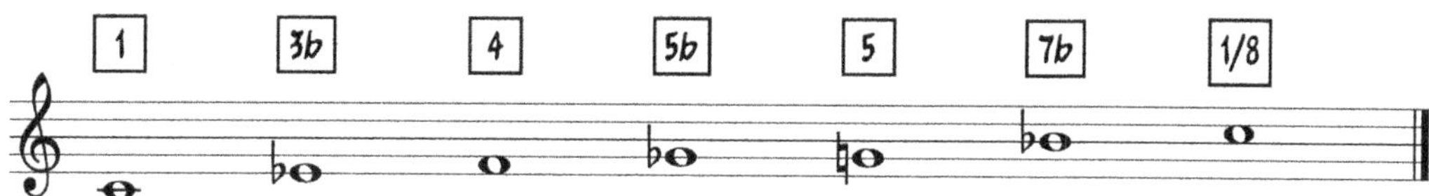

Shown As Named

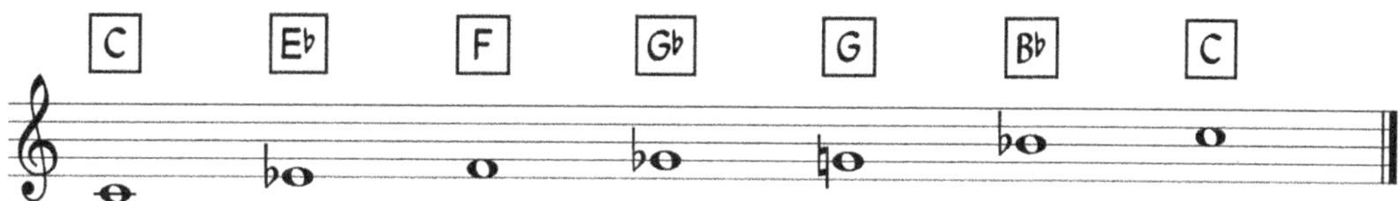

Fingering Suggestion   (Right-Hand)

1.   When not moving any higher.

2.   When continuing on further up.

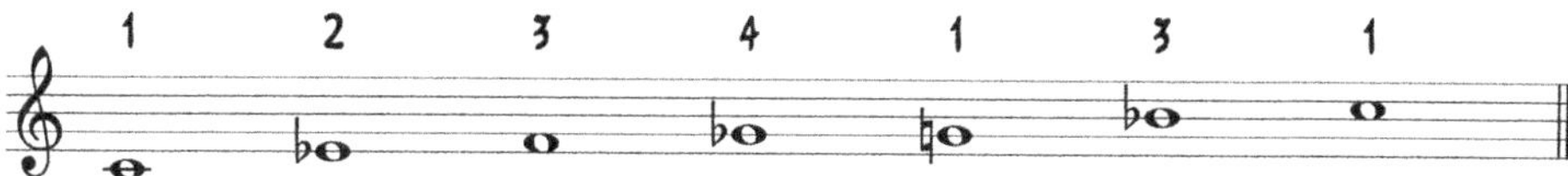

> The thumb (1) is crossed over at the top *if* the scale is to continue on up into another octave, otherwise the little finger (5) can be used at the top.

Db – Minor Blues

The 'Db' minor-blues scale could be considered awkward compared to some, with the three black keys spaced between the whites. Although technically correct, the double-flat shown for the flat-fifth is better written as 'G-natural' and the 'Fb' is generally better written as an 'E', it's cleaner/clearer.

Shown As Degrees

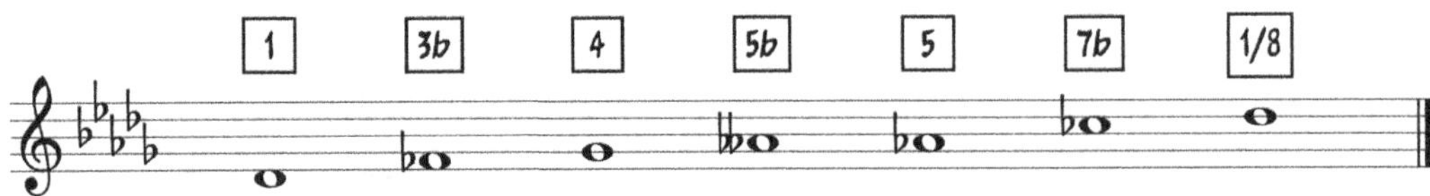

Shown As Named

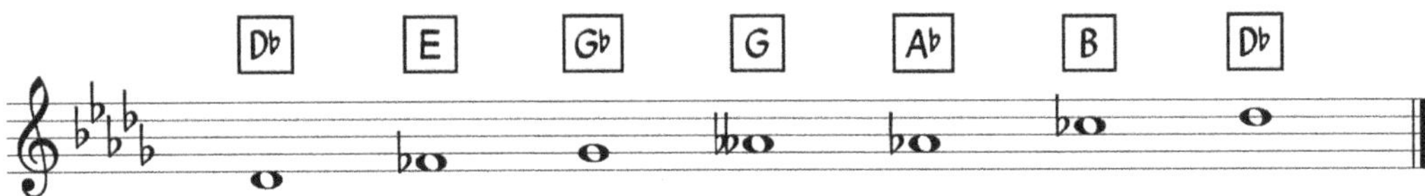

Fingering Suggestion   (Right-Hand)

1.   When not moving any higher.

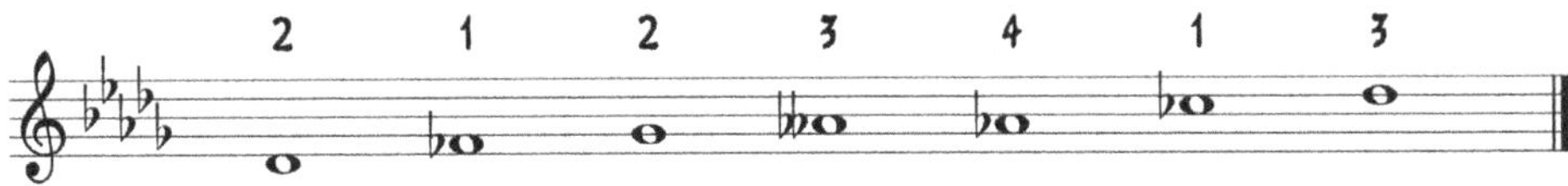

2.   When continuing on further up.

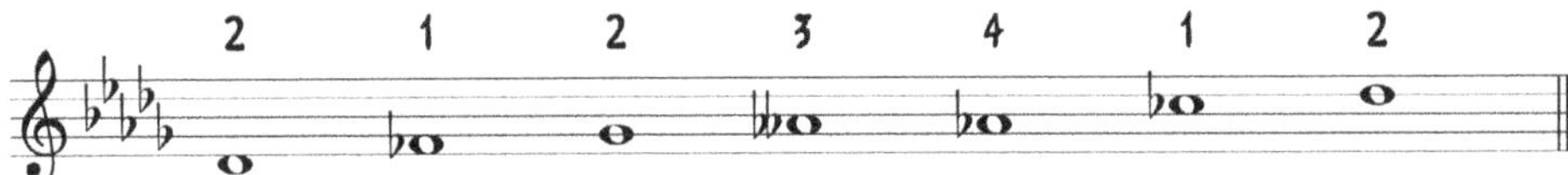

Start on a black key using finger (2). *If* moving continuing up another octave, finger (2) would need to land on the 'Db' to repeat the pattern. If moving no further, then (2) or (3) could be used.

D – Minor Blues

The 'D' minor-blues scale is perhaps one of the nicer versions, with only one black key the scale flows nicely across the keyboard. The pattern (the shape over the key-bed) is similar to the 'A', 'B' and 'E' minor-blues scales.

Shown As Degrees

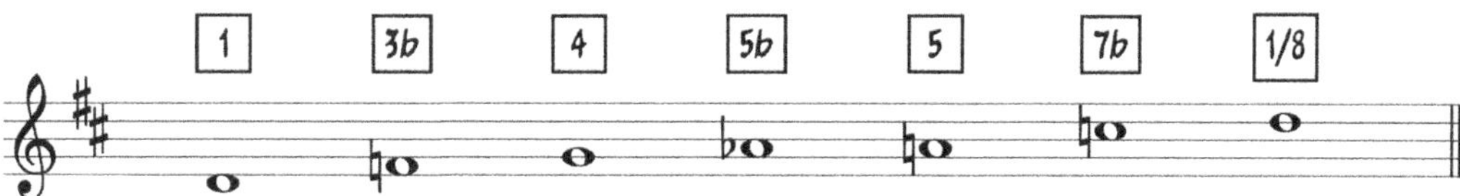

Shown As Named

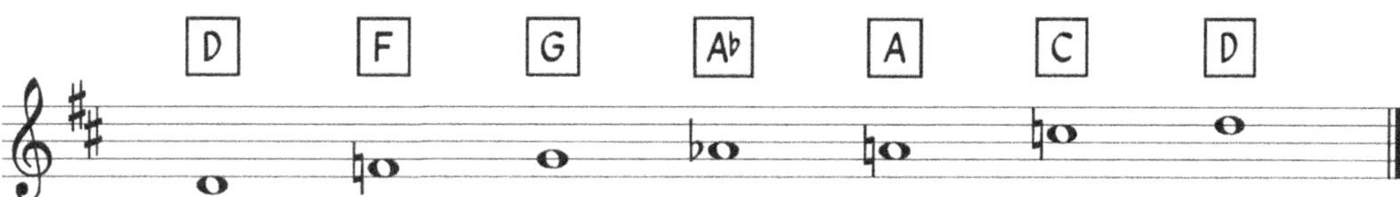

Fingering Suggestion   (Right-Hand)

1.   When not moving any higher.

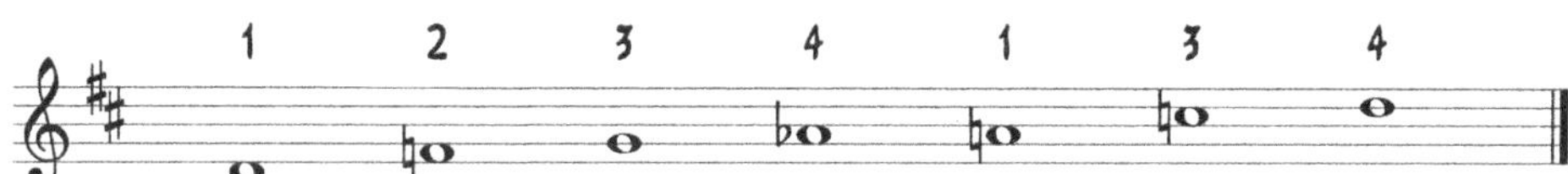

2.   When continuing on further up.

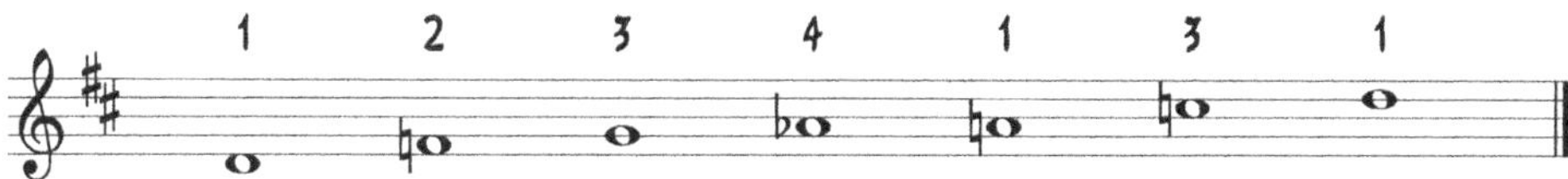

The thumb (1) is crossed over at the top *if* the scale is to continue on up into another octave, otherwise there is no need for the extra movement and finger (4) can be used.

E♭ – Minor Blues

With only one white key and all the black keys in use, this scale is quite easy to remember. Although being nearly all black keys means it is perhaps not the smoothest to play. The 'B-double flat' is likely to notated as an 'A-natural' a lot of the time, as it looks cleaner even though perhaps is not technically correct.

Shown As Degrees

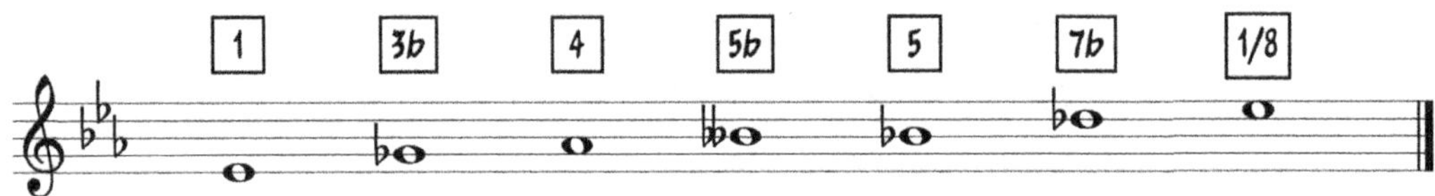

Shown As Named

Fingering Suggestion   (Right-Hand)

1.   When not moving any higher.

2.   When continuing on further up.

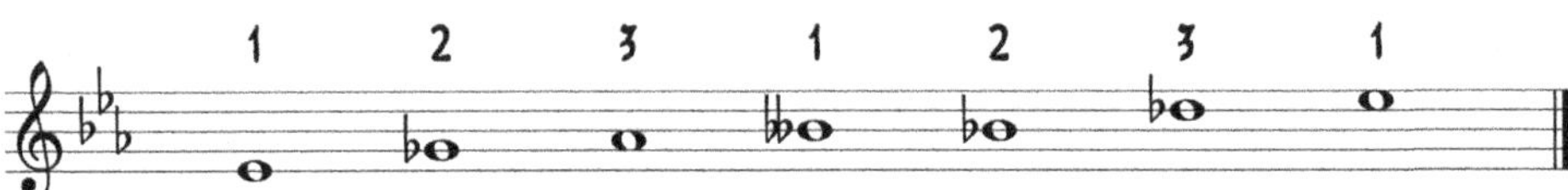

Although starting with a black key, the layout of the scale (predominantly black keys) means it flows better when starting with the thumb. This is crossed over at the top *if* the scale is to continue on up into another octave, otherwise there is no need for the extra movement and finger (4) can be used instead.

E – Minor Blues

The 'E' minor-blues scale is perhaps one of the nicer versions, with only one black key the scale flows nicely across the keyboard. The pattern (the shape over the key-bed) is similar to the 'A', 'B' and 'D' minor-blues scales.

Shown As Degrees

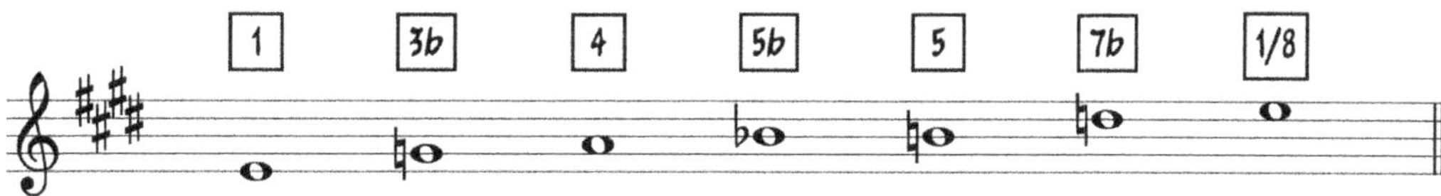

Shown As Named

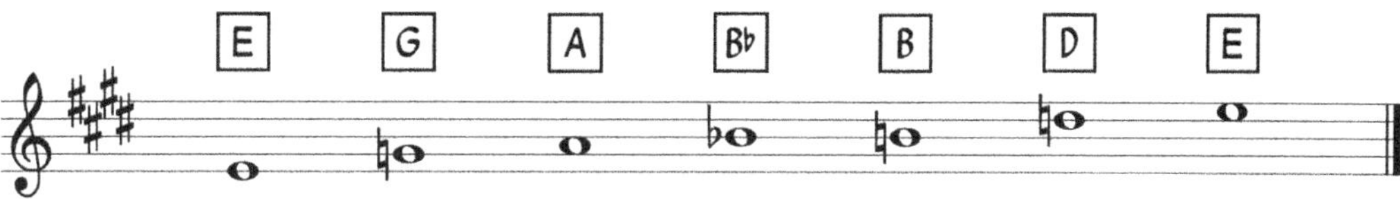

Fingering Suggestion   (Right-Hand)

1.   When not moving any higher.

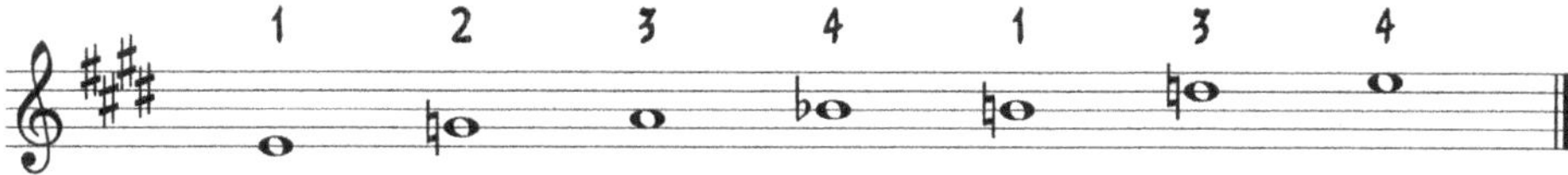

2.   When continuing on further up.

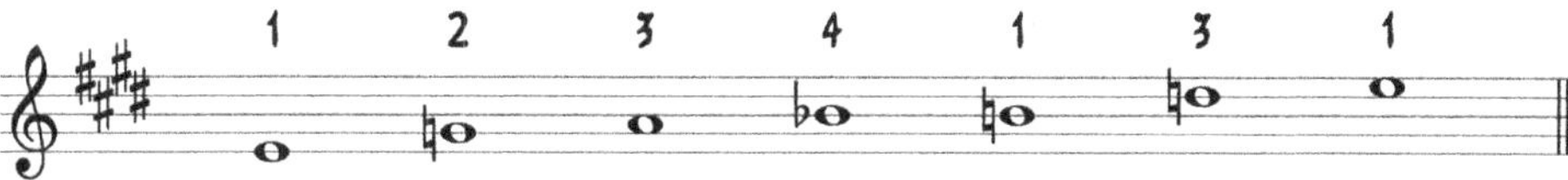

The thumb (1) is crossed over at the top *if* the scale is to continue on up into another octave, otherwise there is no need for the extra movement and finger (4) can be used.

F – Minor Blues

The 'F' minor-blues scale works nicely over the piano key-bed. The flat-fifth although technically a 'C♭' would generally be considered and written as a 'B' for ease.

Shown As Degrees

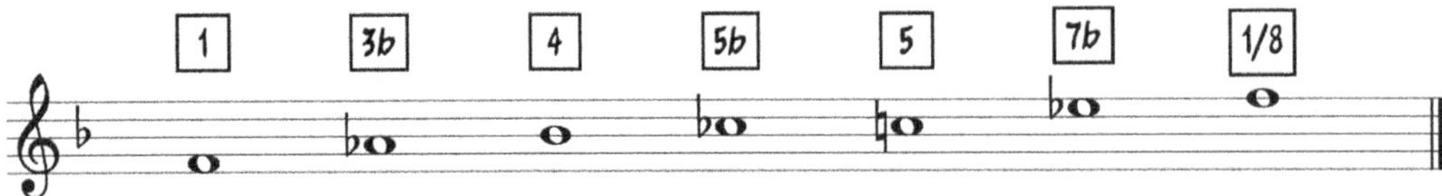

Shown As Named

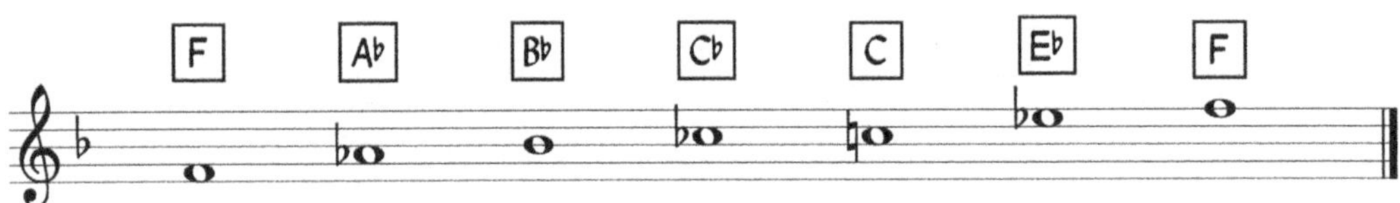

Fingering Suggestion   (Right-Hand)

1.   When not moving any higher.

2.   When continuing on further up.

The thumb (1) is crossed over at the top *if* the scale is to continue on up into another octave, otherwise there is no need for the extra movement and finger (5) can be used.

F♯ – Minor Blues

The 'F♯' minor-blues scale uses three white and two black keys, so a fairly even number. The root note is a black key though which always makes the scale more awkward to play compared to some others.

Shown As Degrees

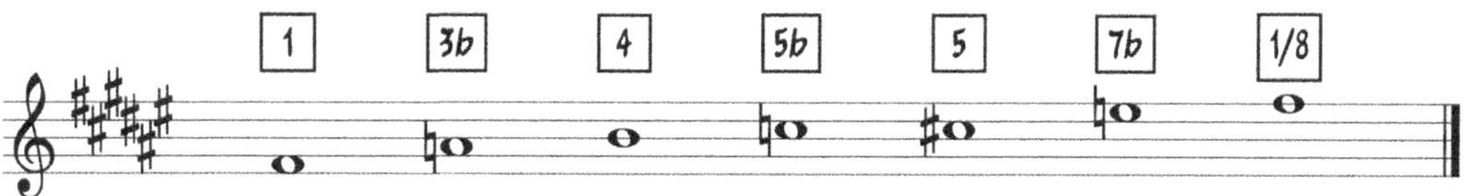

Shown As Named

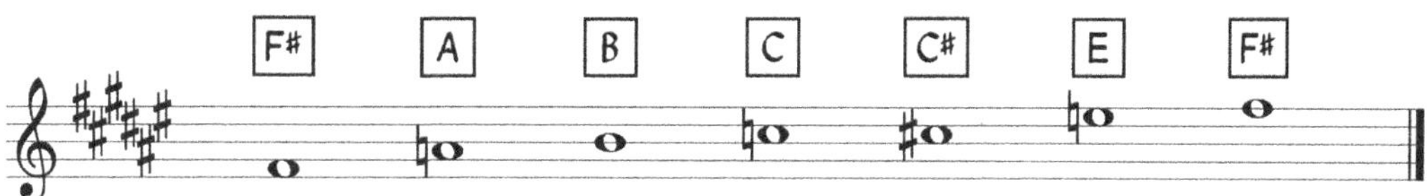

Fingering Suggestion   (Right-Hand)

1.   When not moving any higher.

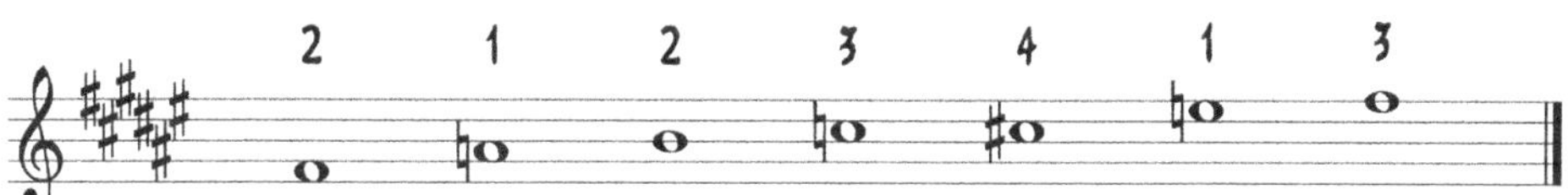

2.   When continuing on further up.

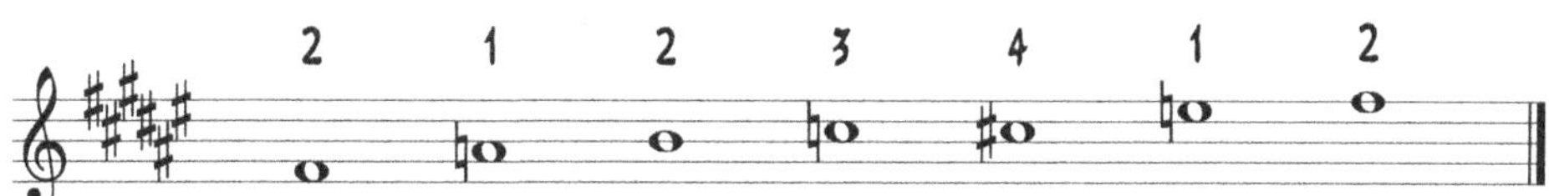

Starting with a black key, we begin with finger (2). This would need to land on the 'F♯' at the top of the scale to repeat the pattern *if* moving on to another octave. If moving no further either (2) or (3) could be used.

G – Minor Blues

The 'G' minor scales shares a similar pattern over the keyboard as the 'E', 'A' and 'D' minor-blues scales, and as such falls under the fingers quite nicely.

Shown As Degrees

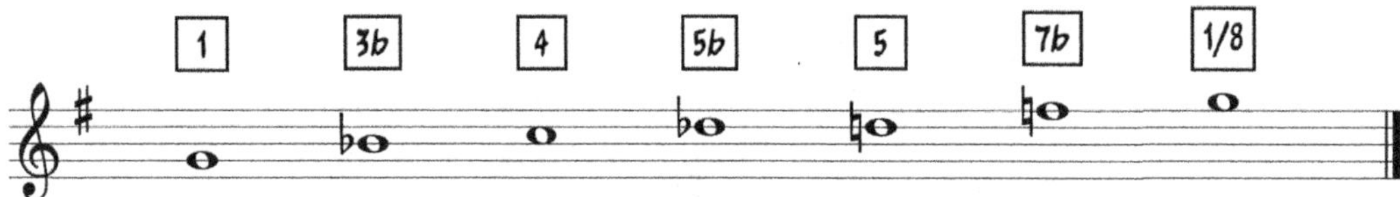

Shown As Named

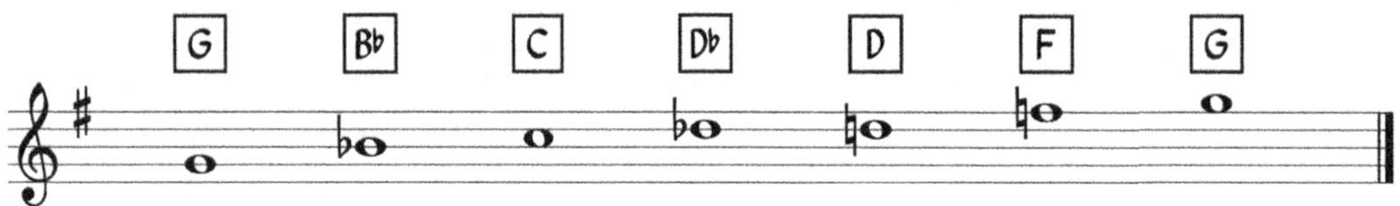

Fingering Suggestion   (Right-Hand)

1.   When not moving any higher.

2.   When continuing on further up.

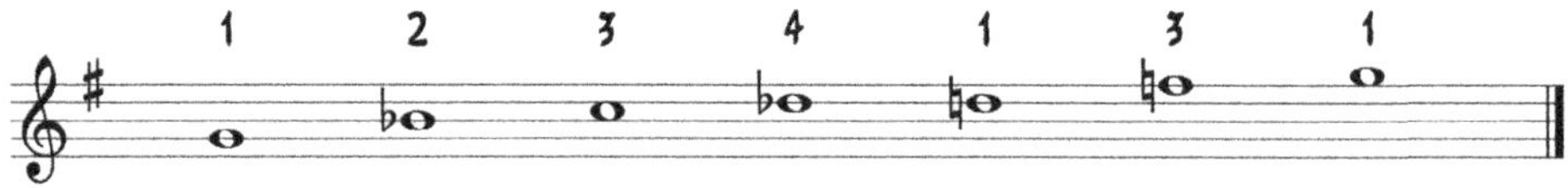

The thumb (1) is crossed over at the top *if* the scale is to continue on up into another octave, otherwise there is no need for the extra movement and finger (2) can be used.

A♭ – Minor Blues

The 'A♭' minor-blues scale has four black keys, so like most of the flat keys it is more awkward to play. The 'C♭' is more likely to be notated as a 'B-natural' and the double flat is never popular, so more likely to be shown as a 'D-natural'. It's less messy and easier for everyone to read.

Shown As Degrees

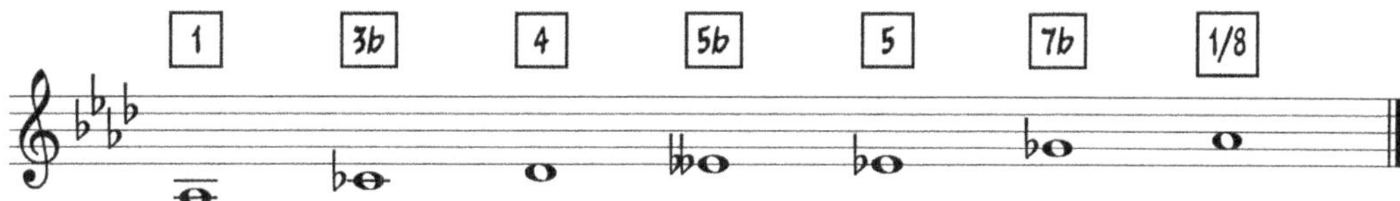

Shown As Named

Fingering Suggestion   (Right-Hand)

1.   When not moving any higher.

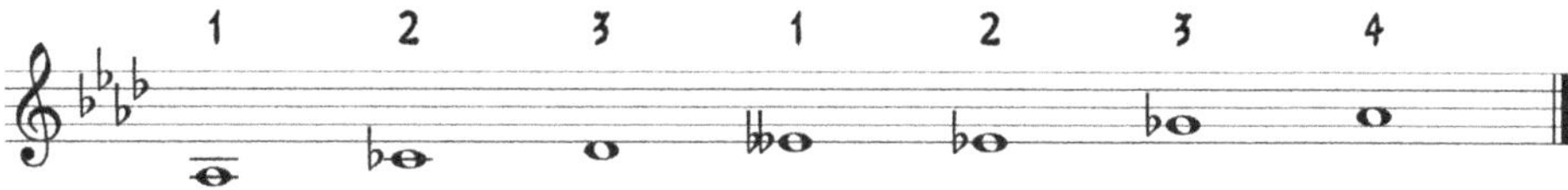

2.   When continuing on further up.

Although common practice to not start with the thumb on a black key, the blues scales break a few rules (or rather there are none) and this key works better when starting with the thumb (1). Experiment yourself and see what works best for you.

Major-Blues Scales

A – Major Blues

The 'A' major blues scale doesn't flow quite as well as the minor-blues scale, as it uses two black keys as opposed to the one found in the minor version.

Shown As Degrees

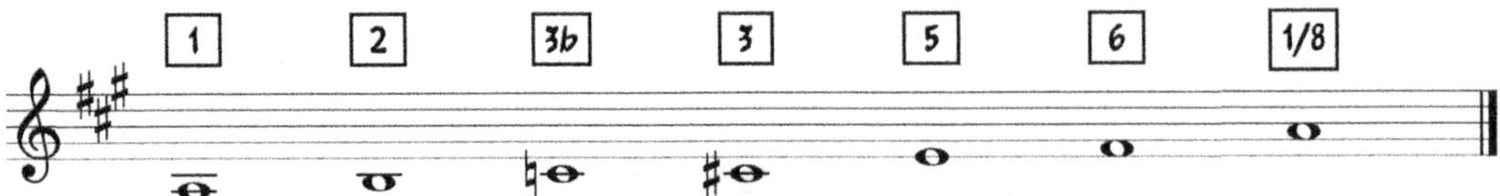

Shown As Named

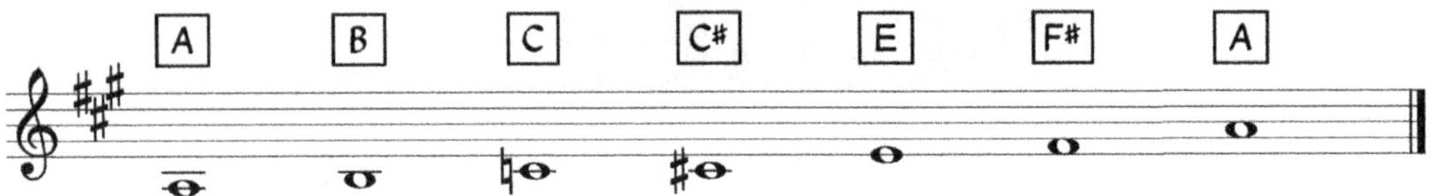

Fingering Suggestions   (Right-Hand)

1.   When not moving any higher.

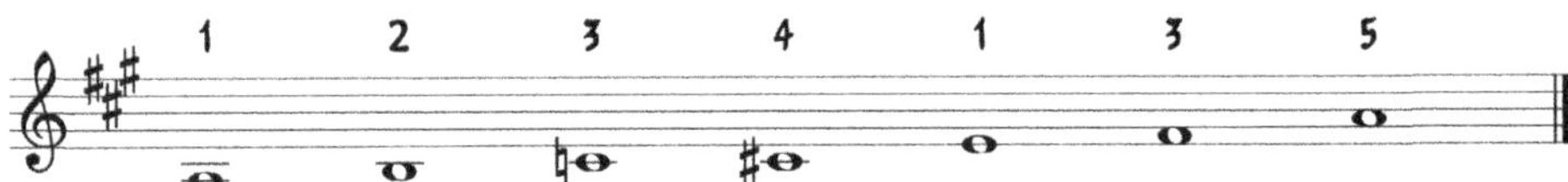

2.   When continuing on further up.

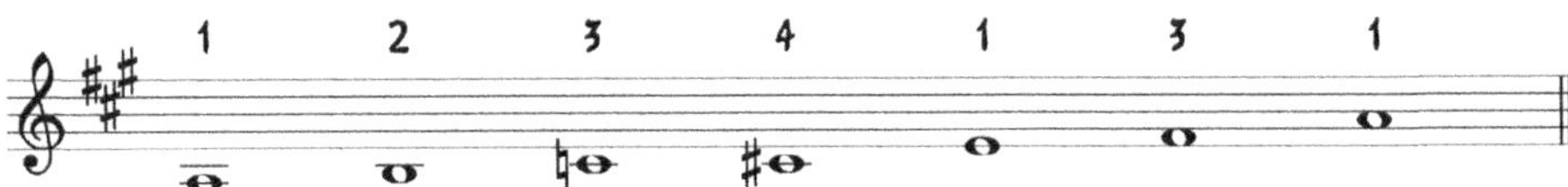

The thumb (1) is crossed over at the top *if* the scale is to continue on up into another octave, otherwise the little finger (5) can be used at the top.

B♭ – Major Blues

The 'B♭' major blues scale uses two black keys so isn't too bad to remember, although it does begin on a black key, which always makes the fingering a little more awkward.

Shown As Degrees

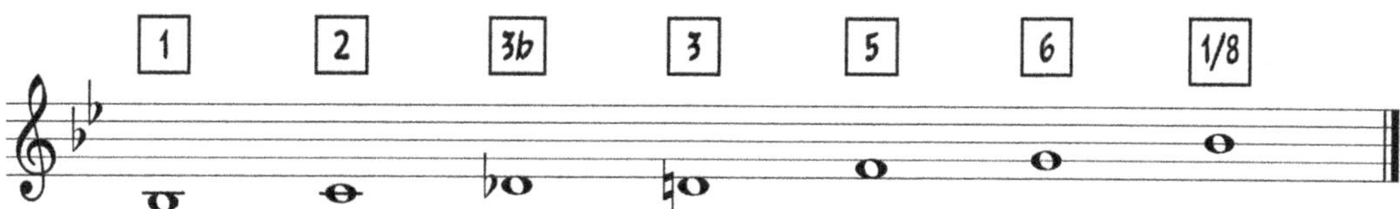

Shown As Named

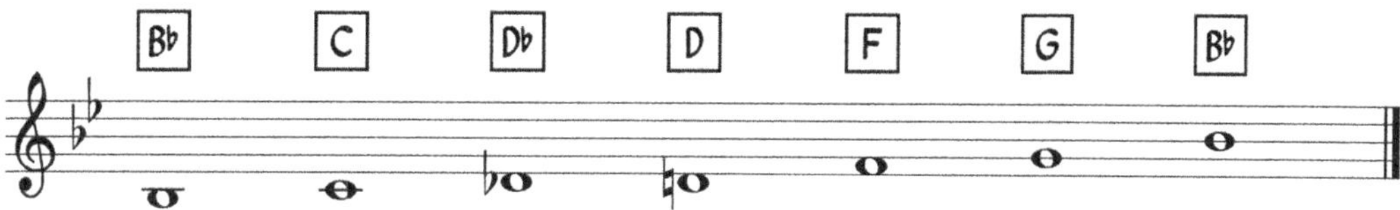

Fingering Suggestions   (Right-Hand)

1.   When not moving any higher.

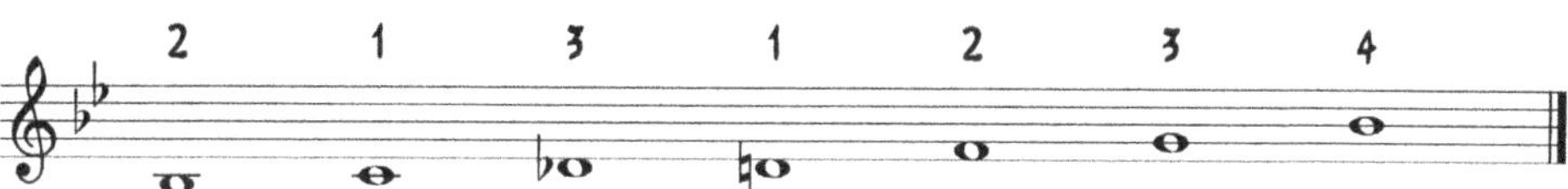

2.   When continuing on further up.

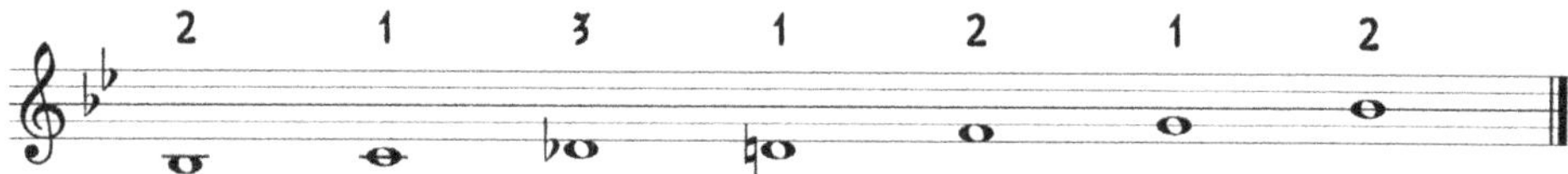

Starting with a black key, we begin with finger (2). This would need to land on the 'B♭' at the top of the scale to repeat the pattern *if* moving on to another octave. If moving no further either (4) could be used.

B – Major Blues

The 'B' major blues scale is predominately black keys with only two white. It doesn't exactly flow nicely, but at least it starts on a white key which helps, although the fingering is relatively awkward compared to some keys.

Shown As Degrees

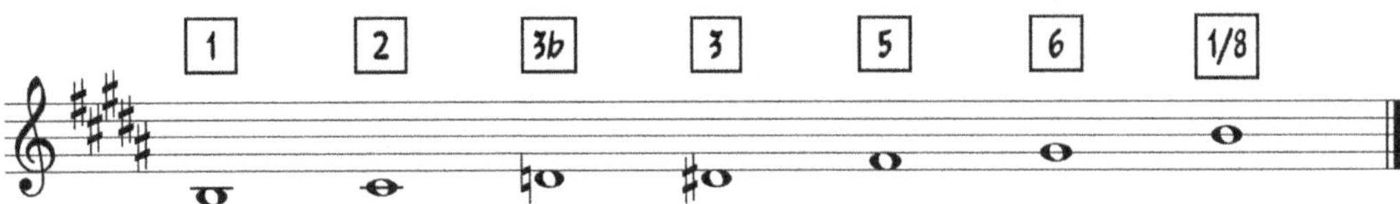

Shown As Named

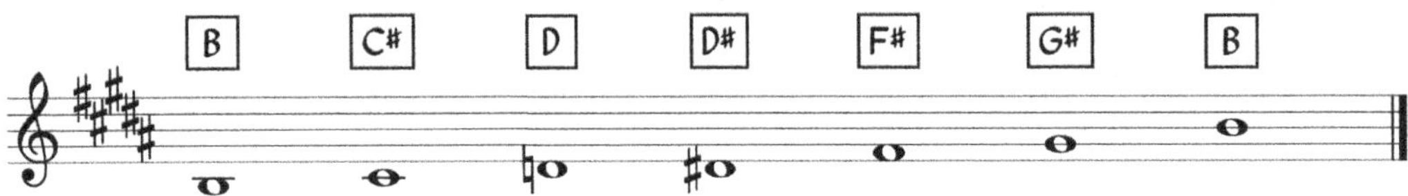

Fingering Suggestions   (Right-Hand)

1.   When not moving any higher.

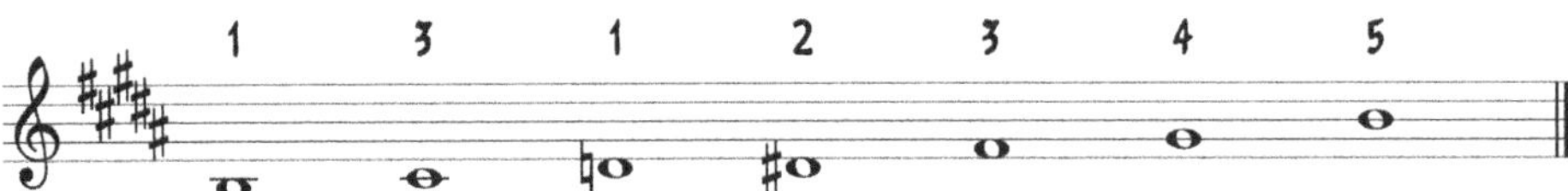

2.   When continuing on further up.

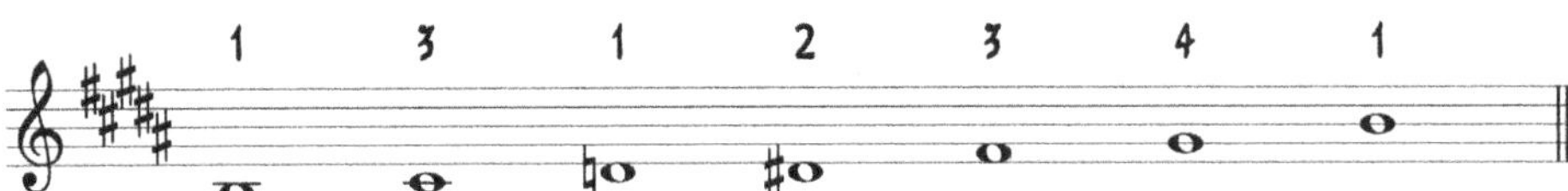

The thumb (1) is crossed over at the top *if* the scale is to continue on up into another octave, otherwise the little finger (5) can be used at the top.

C – Major Blues

The 'C' major-blues scale fits quite nicely under your fingers with only one flat (a black key) to contend with.

Shown As Degrees

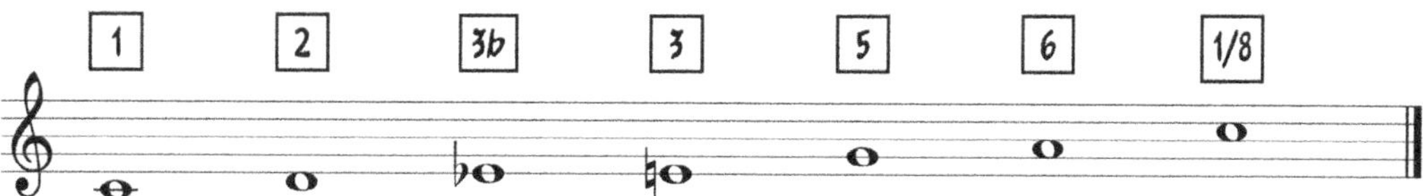

Shown As Named

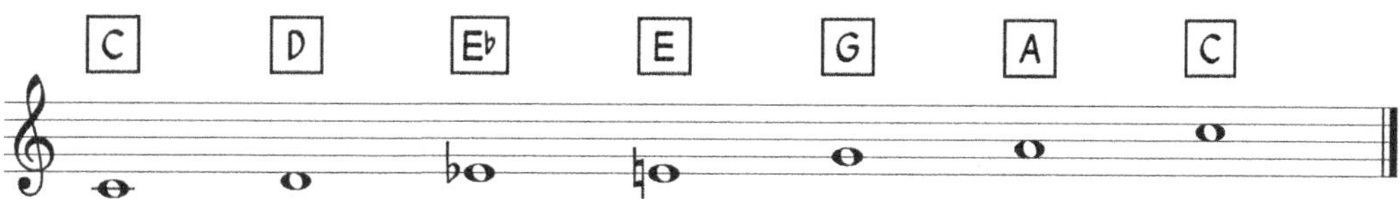

Fingering Suggestions   (Right-Hand)

1.   When not moving any higher.

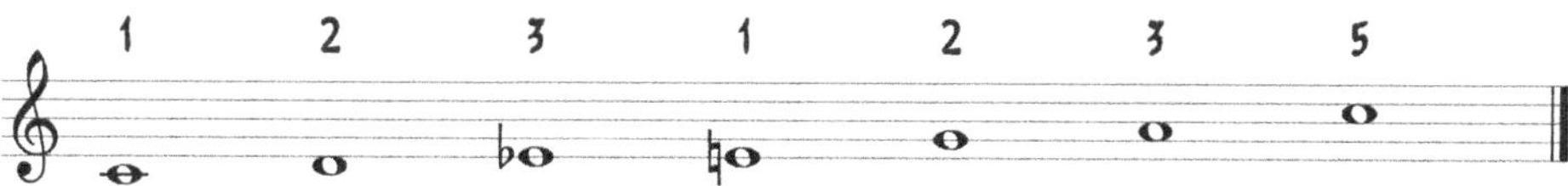

2.   When continuing on further up.

The thumb (1) is crossed over at the top *if* the scale is to continue on up into another octave, otherwise the little finger (5) can be used at the top.

D♭ – Major Blues

The 'D♭' major-blues scale contains twice as many black keys compared to white, making the fingering trickier than you might like. It starts with a black key which changes the fingering somewhat, which never exactly flows freely.

Shown As Degrees

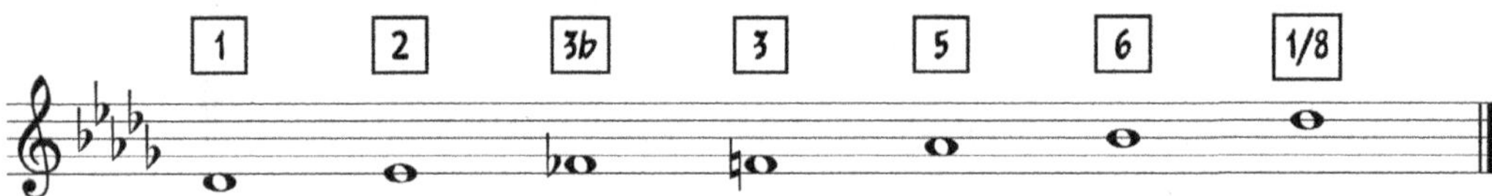

Shown As Named

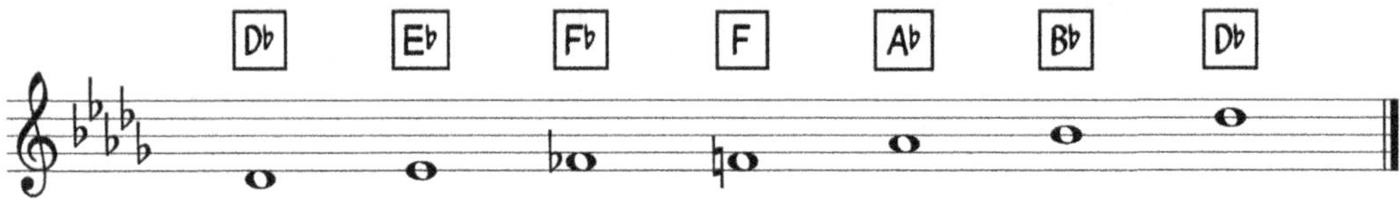

Fingering Suggestions   (Right-Hand)

1. When not moving any higher.

2. When continuing on further up.

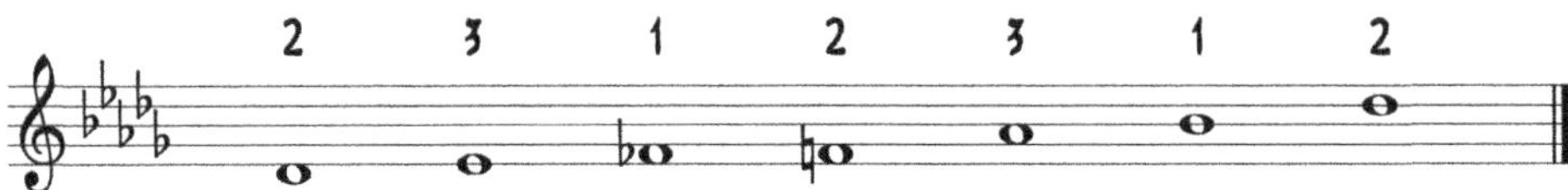

Starting with finger (2), the thumb (1) is crossed over at the top *if* the scale is to continue on up into another octave, otherwise fingers (4) and (5) can be used at the top. Although awkward, it's possible to start with the thumb instead, that said the fingering for this one is awkward regardless.

D – Major Blues

The 'D' major-blues scale is quite a nice one, with only one black key to contend with it flows nicely with no awkward points on the keyboard.

Shown As Degrees

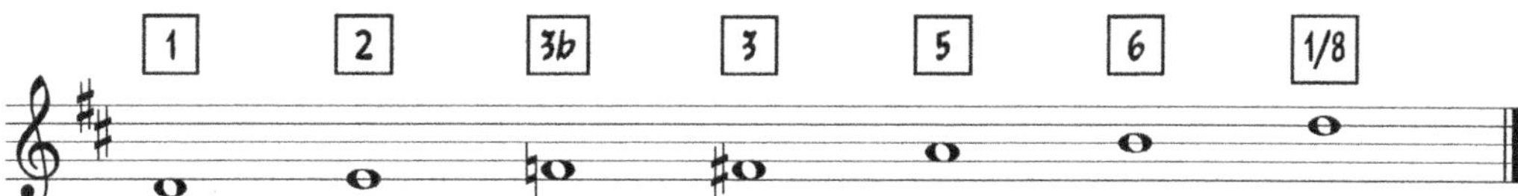

Shown As Named

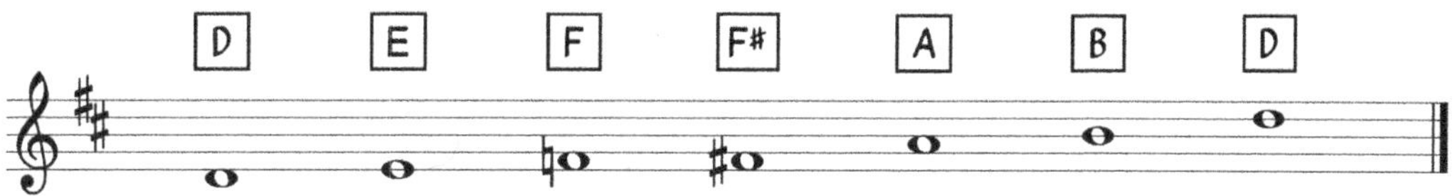

Fingering Suggestions   (Right-Hand)

1.   When not moving any higher.

2.   When continuing on further up.

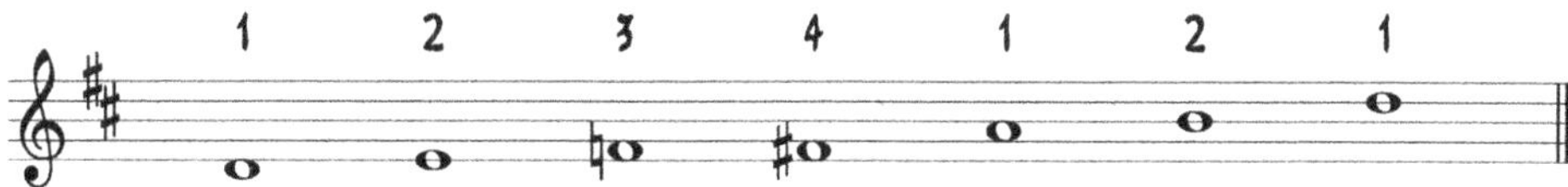

The thumb (1) is crossed over at the top *if* the scale is to continue on up into another octave, otherwise finger (4) can be used at the top.

E♭ – Major Blues

The 'E♭' major-blues scale is spread equally between black and white keys which are spaced quite evenly, making it perhaps one of the nicer flat keys to work with.

Shown As Degrees

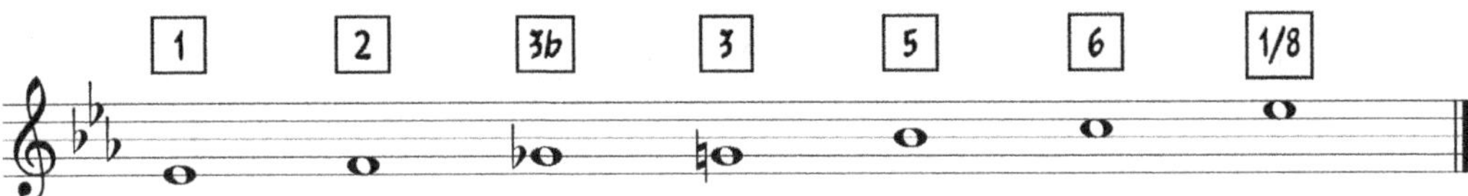

Shown As Named

Fingering Suggestions   (Right-Hand)

1.   When not moving any higher.

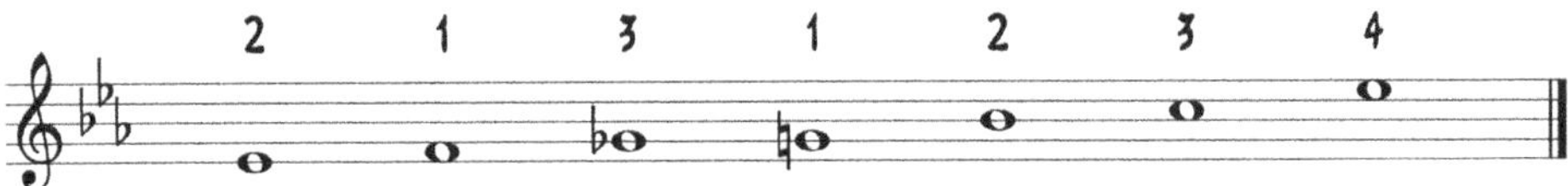

2.   When continuing on further up.

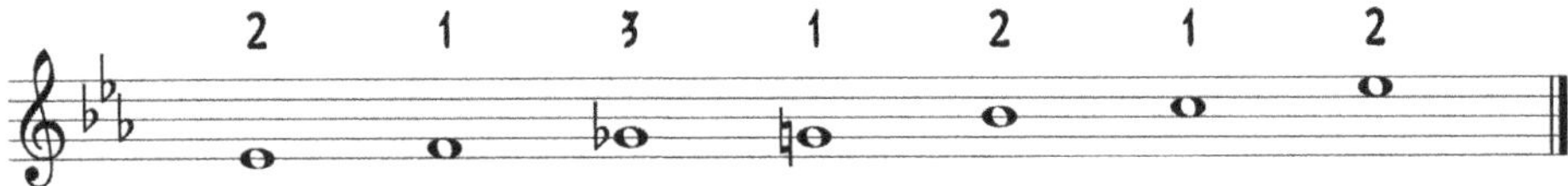

With the root being a black key this is best started with finger (2). Fingers (1) and (2) are used at the top *if* the scale is to continue up an octave, otherwise fingers (3) and (4) can be used at the top.

E – Major Blues

The 'E' major-blues scale is even spread between the black and white keys and doesn't flow anywhere near as nicely as the minor version. There are a couple of ways you might play this, the one shown is probably the quickest.

Shown As Degrees

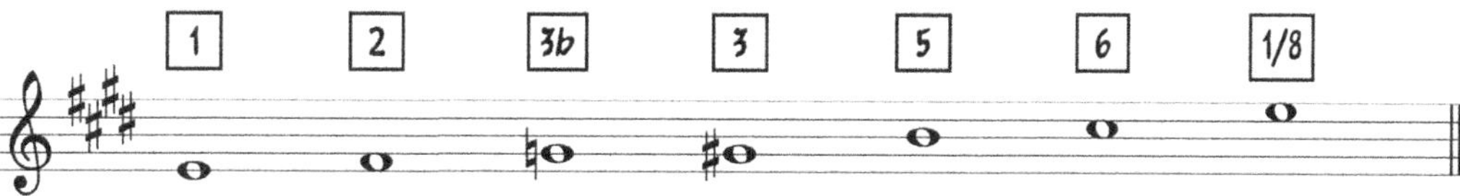

Shown As Named

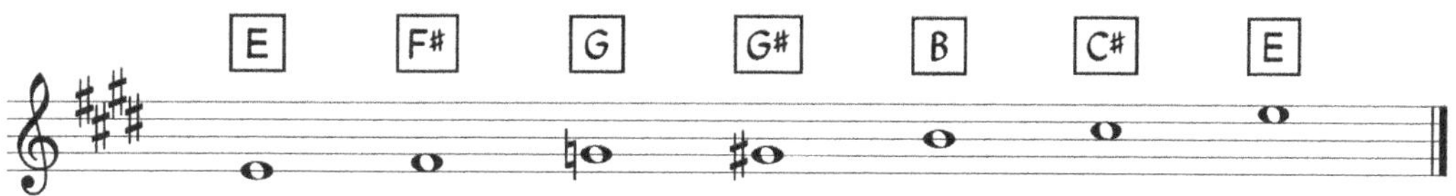

Fingering Suggestions   (Right-Hand)

1.   When not moving any higher.

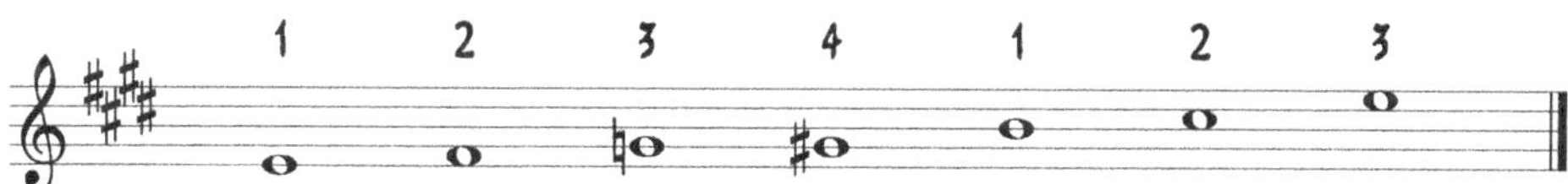

2.   When continuing on further up.

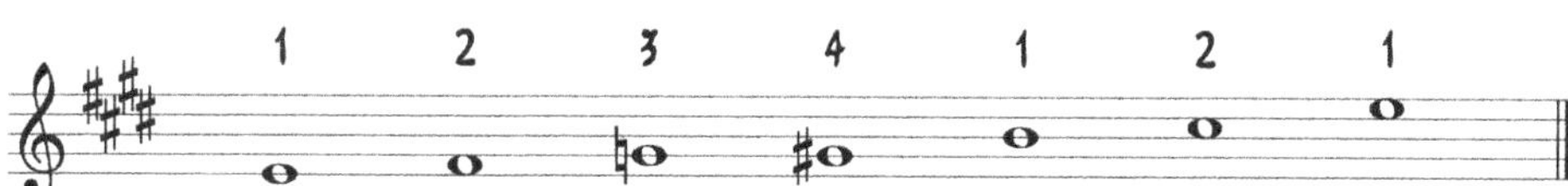

The thumb (1) is crossed over at the top *if* the scale is to continue on up into another octave, otherwise finger (3) can be used at the top.

Alternatively finger (3) could be substituted on the 'C#' if you prefer (feels more natural to me, chose whatever feels best to you).

F – Major Blues

The 'F' major-blues scale plays very nicely with only one black key to contend with, making it one of the more pleasant keys for the major version.

Shown As Degrees

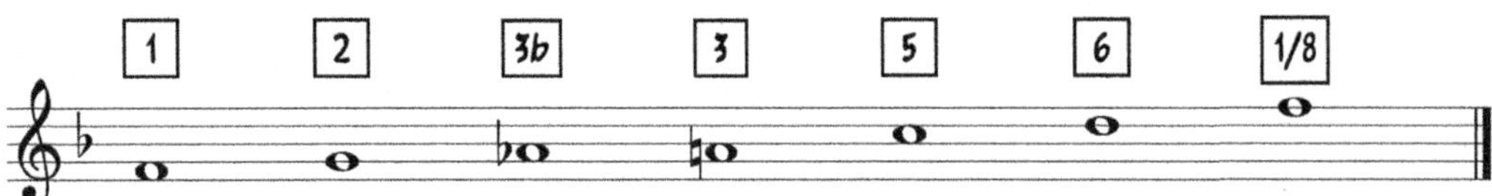

Shown As Named

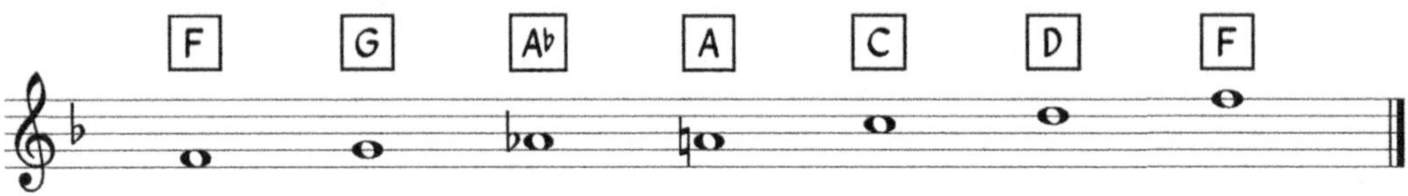

Fingering Suggestions   (Right-Hand)

1.   When not moving any higher.

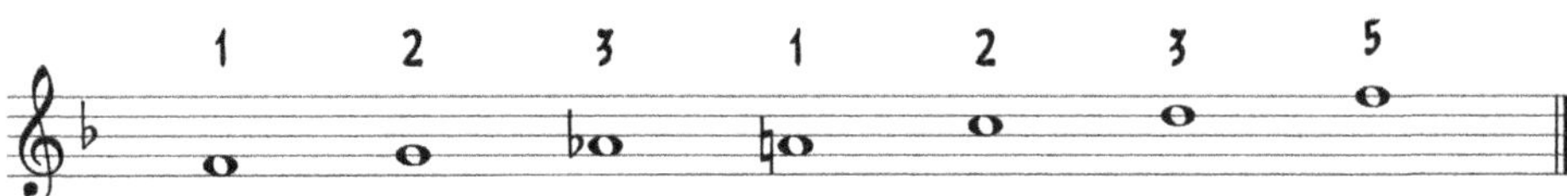

2.   When continuing on further up.

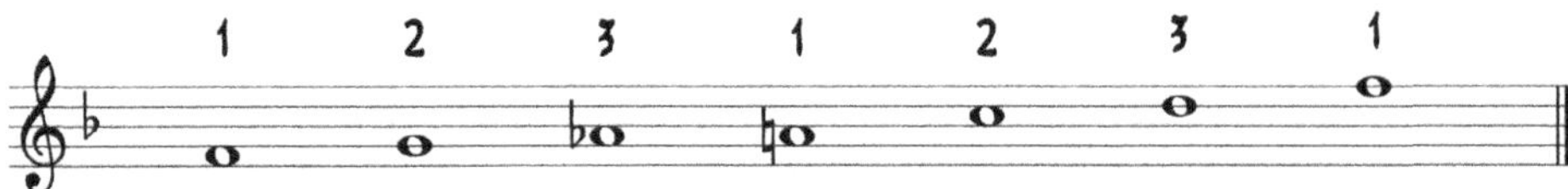

The thumb (1) is crossed over at the top *if* the scale is to continue on up into another octave, otherwise the little finger (5) can be used at the top.

F♯ – Major Blues

The 'F♯' major-blues scale only uses one white key which make it quite easy to remember, although perhaps more difficult to play because of this.

Shown As Degrees

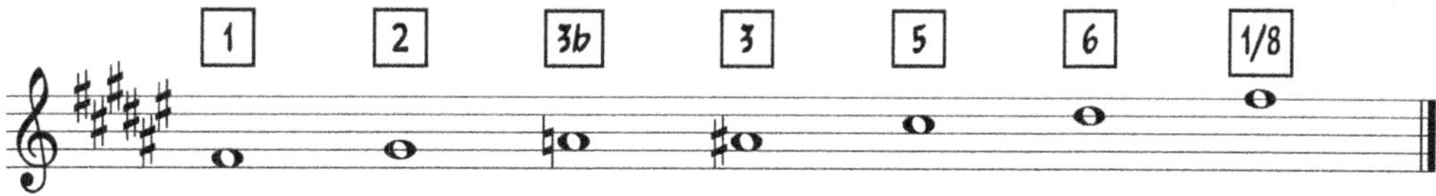

Shown As Named

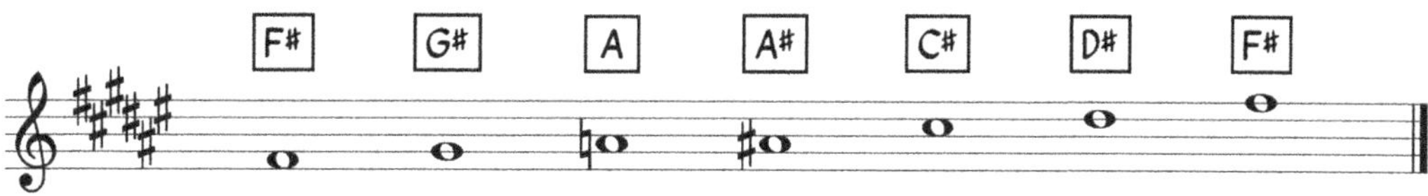

Fingering Suggestions   (Right-Hand)

1.   When not moving any higher.

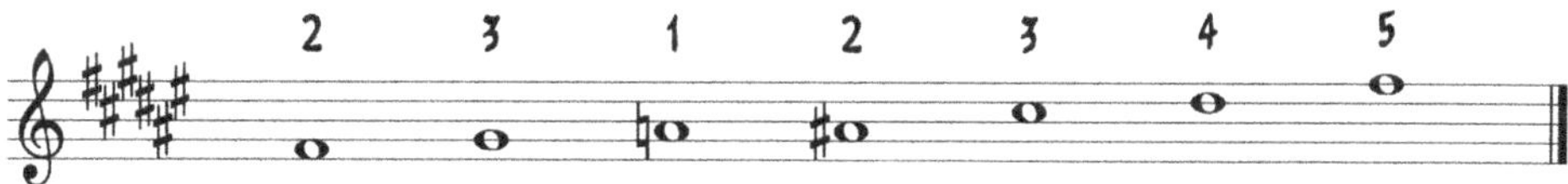

2.   When continuing on further up.

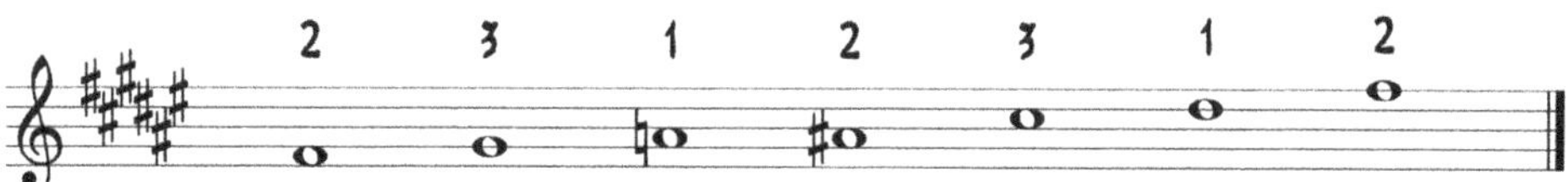

Beginning on a black key, it's recommended to start with finger (2). If you are to end on the root note, then moving up through all the fingers can work. If moving up another octave, then you need to cross the thumb(1) onto the 'D♯' so that you can get finger (2) back onto the root note.

G – Major Blues

The 'G' major-blues only uses one flat which make it easy to remember and nice to play as it flows over the keyboard quite freely, not surprising really as this key works very well for blues on the piano.

Shown As Degrees

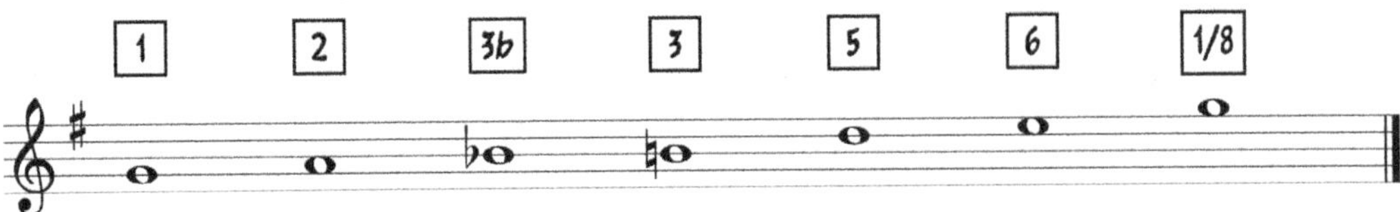

Shown As Named

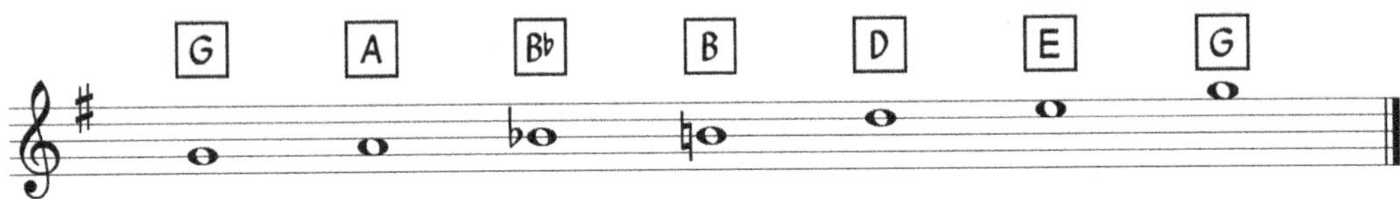

Fingering Suggestions   (Right-Hand)

1.   When not moving any higher.

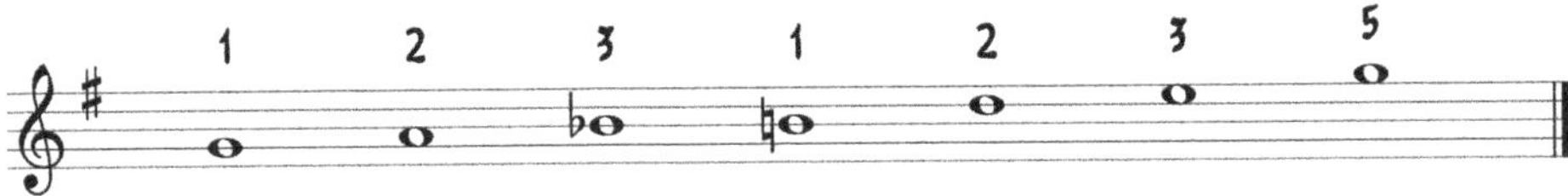

2.   When continuing on further up.

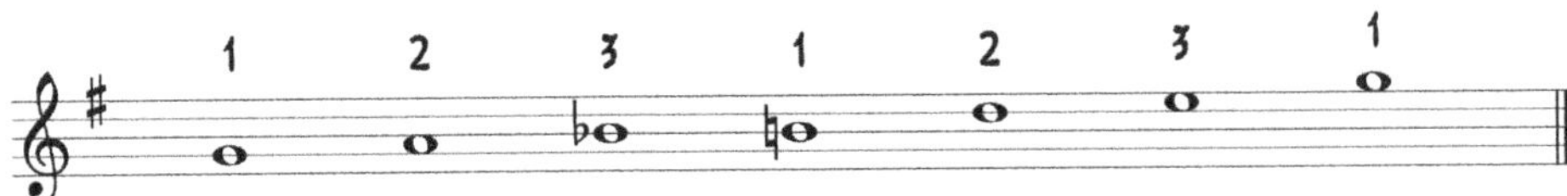

> The thumb (1) is crossed over at the top *if* the scale is to continue on up into another octave, otherwise the little finger (5) can be used at the top.

A♭ – Major Blues

The 'A♭' major-blues scale is split equally between black and white keys. For a flat-key it is perhaps one of the better flowing examples and the fingering is relatively simple.

Shown As Degrees

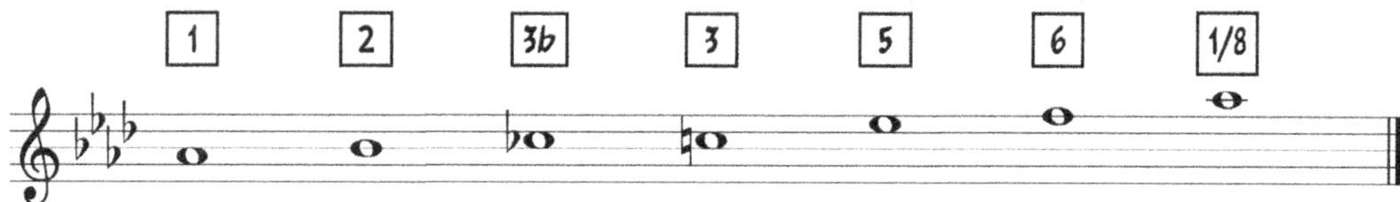

Shown As Named

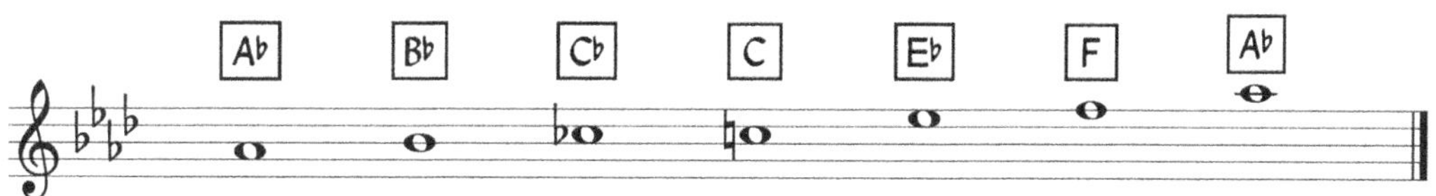

Fingering Suggestions   (Right-Hand)

1.   When not moving any higher.

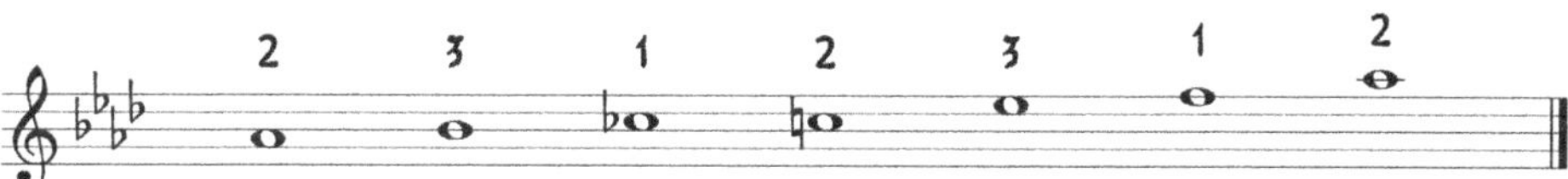

2.   When continuing on further up.

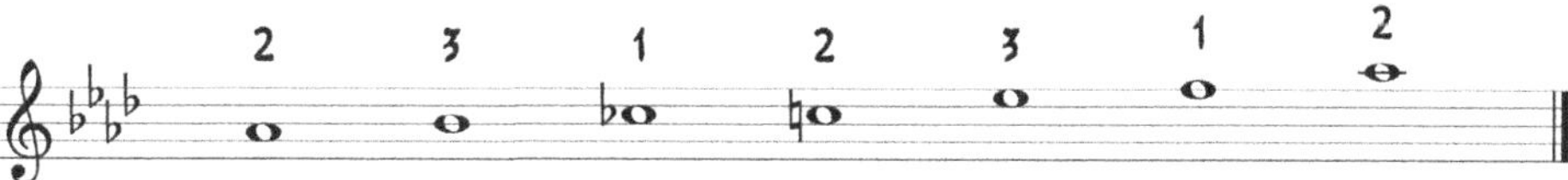

This scale begins on a black key, so it's recommended to start with finger (2). You can see the same fingering for both continuing up and no, as there's no real advantage to changing it. You could potentially use finger (3) on the top root note (if not moving further up), but then why complicate it.

Combined Blues Scales

What Is The Combined Scale

Before we go any further, I must point out that what we are referring to as a combined scale isn't a true scale in the normal sense of the word. The blues scales themselves aren't considered to be real in traditional music theory, so this most certainly won't be, but, in practical terms this can be a useful way of thinking for a blues based player. It's from a very well respected blues/rock pianist that I myself took this idea from some years ago. It certainly begins to help prevent getting stuck in the 'blues-scale' loop, where you never play outside of the scale, which can become quite limiting.

The combined scale simply takes both the major and minor blues scales and combines them into one. This can be used in a manner of ways, being a useful addition to your tool box. It's important to know the two scales as individual entities first though, certainly getting to know them very well before you consider combining them.

Used In Its Entirety

Using the scale in its entirety (running up or down etc.), while the scale can be used like this it doesn't always fit in all situations. You'll be-able to hear this yourself when you play one through, it works in some contexts while sometimes not, with practice you'll be-able to judge how and when you might use it in its entirety.

Pick And Choose From The Tool Box

Here is where it becomes more useful, rather than using the entire scale, think of it like an artists' palette of colours that you can pick and choose from depending on what you need in a given situation. So while improvising a solo (for instance) these are the notes you have to pick from, this actually only leaves three notes that you will avoid, as these are quite dissonant and require very careful use.

Combined Scale Fingering

The combined scales include fingering suggestions, but I must stress that these are just suggestions and may or may not suit you personally. Seeing as the idea of the combined scale is to think of it as a palette of options, in reality you will be using all manner of combinations, so learning a strict fingering structure isn't practical. It helps to learn a few basic rules/ideas, and then learn to become free and open with your fingering, using whatever is available to make your improvisation happen.

Combined Scales Basics

Combined-Blues Scale

This combination of the two blues scales creates a useful palette of options to use while improvising. You should know the two scales separately of course, but learning this helps you move outside the basic blues-scales, which can sometimes be overused and sound stale. It's important to move outside each of these scales and this is a good way to start to do that, having additional notes internalized and ready to drop in at any time.

You end up with a ten note scale (including the repeat of the root note) it consists of the root, second, flat-third, third, fourth, flat-fifth, fifth, sixth and flat-seventh, being degrees of a major scale.

An alternative way of looking at its construction, would be to simply play all the notes except the flat-second, flat-sixth and major-seventh. You could perhaps consider the intervals between notes, although being as there are few gaps, this isn't the best approach.

Degrees Of Major Scale

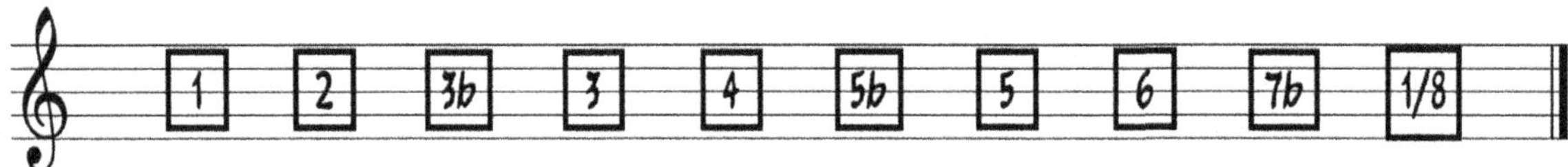

Intervals Used Moving Through The Scale

Whole	Half	Half	Half	Half	Half	Whole	Half	Whole

Combination Examples

Here are a few examples of the two scales being combined in a practical setting, this is just to give you the idea of how the two might work together in practice.

Example No. 1

This is predominantly the major-blues scale, but with the addition of the flat-seventh coming in on the second bar.

Example No. 2

This is predominantly the minor-blues scale, but with the addition of the second (or ninth if you prefer) being used in passing between the root and flat-third.

A – Combined Scale

Practice over one octave to begin with, once comfortable with it, you can then extend the range to two and even three octaves.

Shown As Degrees

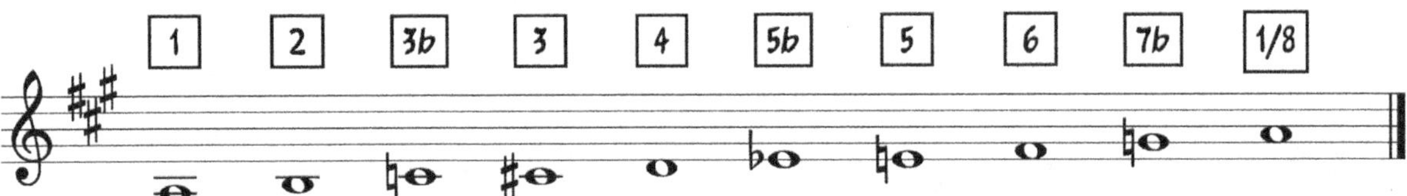

Shown As Named

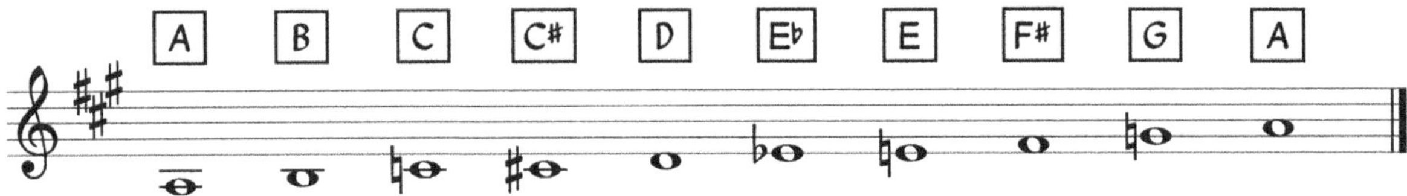

Fingering Suggestions   (Right-Hand)

1.   When not moving any higher.

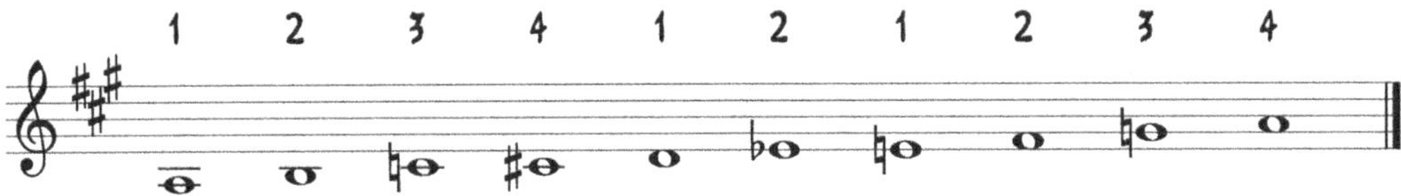

2.   When continuing on further up.

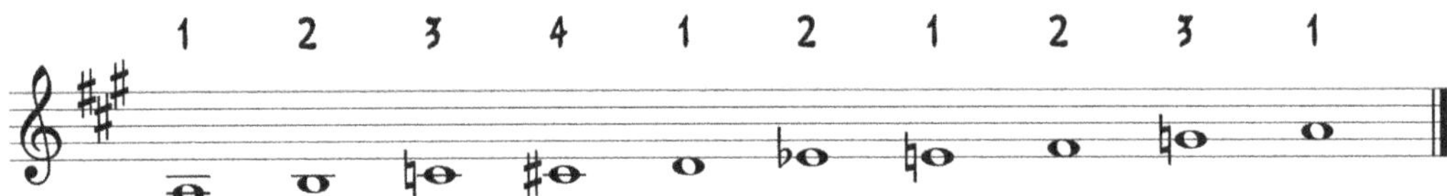

The thumb (1) is crossed over at the top *if* the scale is to continue on up into another octave, otherwise finger (4) could be used at the top.

B♭ – Combined Scale

Practice over one octave to begin with, once comfortable with it, you can then extend the range to two and even three octaves.

Shown As Degrees

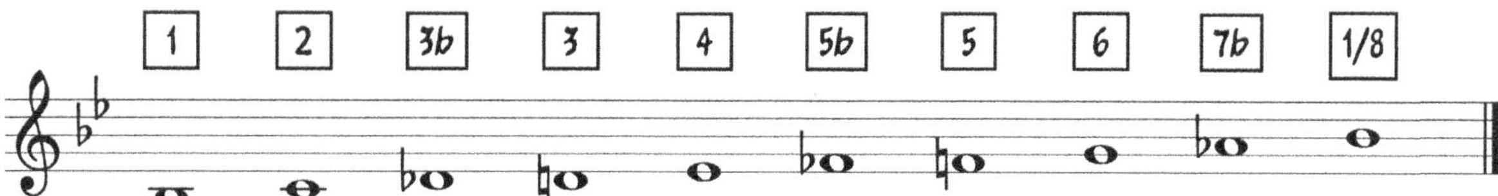

Shown As Named

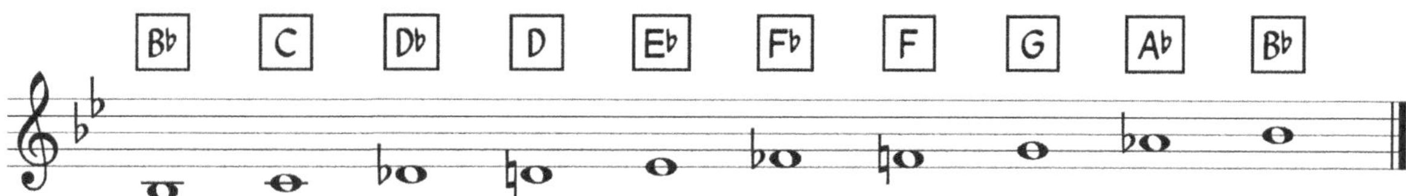

Fingering Suggestions   (Right-Hand)

1.   When not moving any higher.

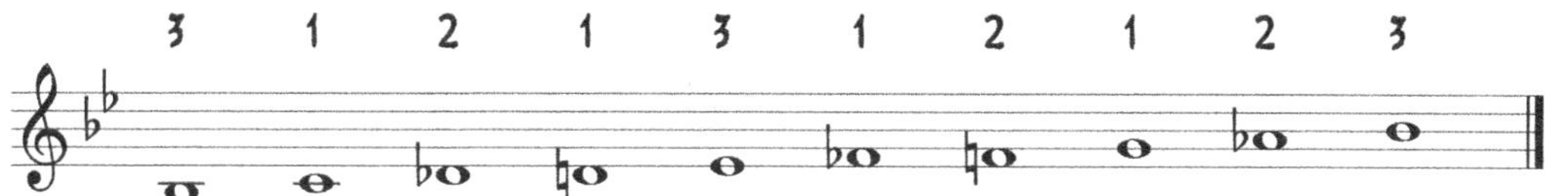

2.   When continuing on further up.

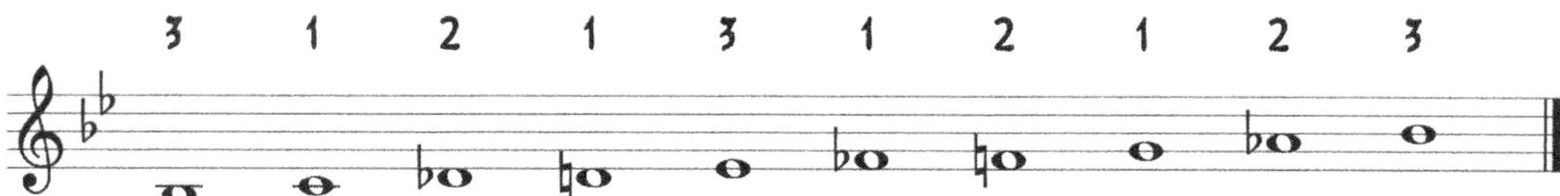

Due to the awkward nature of this one the same fingering is probably best used regardless as to if it ends or continues further into a second octave.

B – Combined Scale

Practice over one octave to begin with, once comfortable with it, you can then extend the range to two and even three octaves.

Shown As Degrees

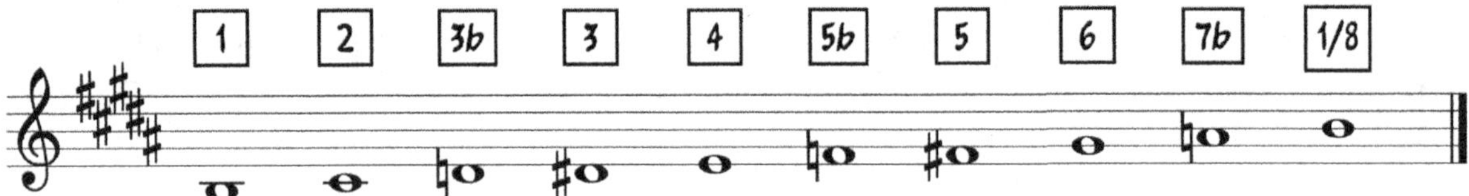

Shown As Named

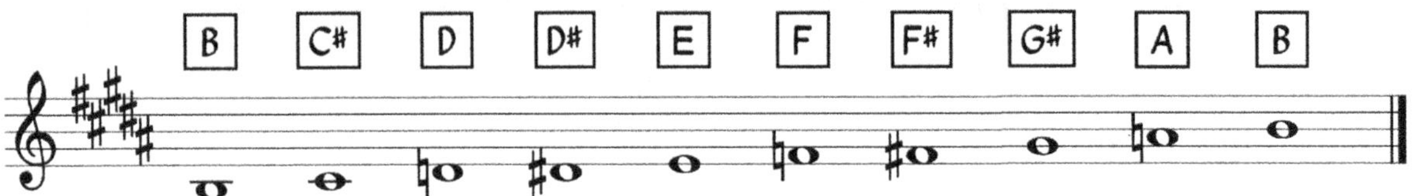

Fingering Suggestions   (Right-Hand)

1.   When not moving any higher.

2.   When continuing on further up.

Due to the awkward nature of this one the same fingering is probably best used regardless as to if it ends or continues further into a second octave.

C – Combined Scale

Practice over one octave to begin with, once comfortable with it, you can then extend the range to two and even three octaves.

Shown As Degrees

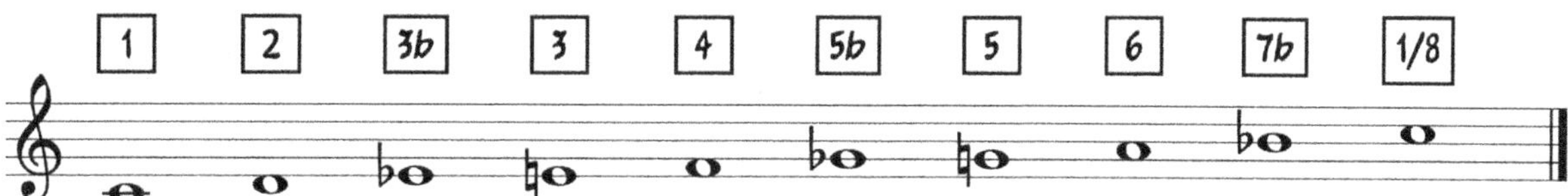

Shown As Named

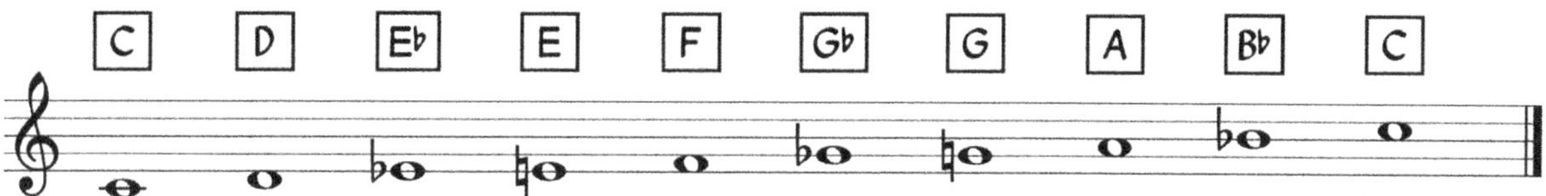

Fingering Suggestions (Right-Hand)

1.   When not moving any higher.

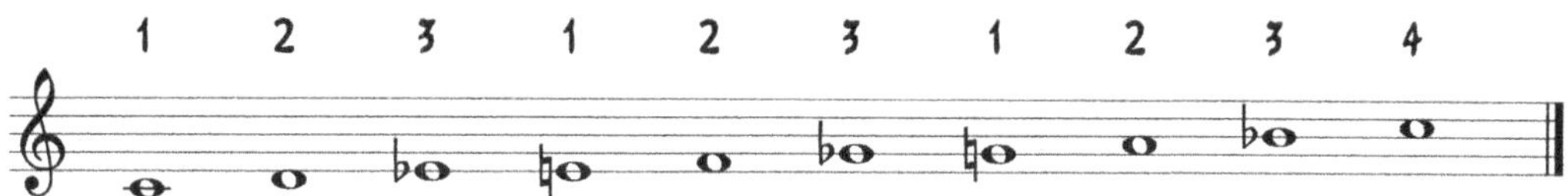

2.   When continuing on further up.

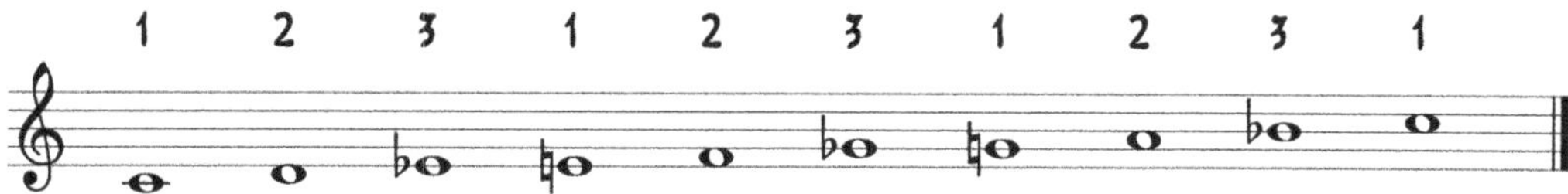

The thumb (1) is crossed over at the top to land back on the root *if* the scale is to continue on into another octave, otherwise finger (4) could be used at the top.

D♭ – Combined Scale

Practice over one octave to begin with, once comfortable with it, you can then extend the range to two and even three octaves.

Shown As Degrees

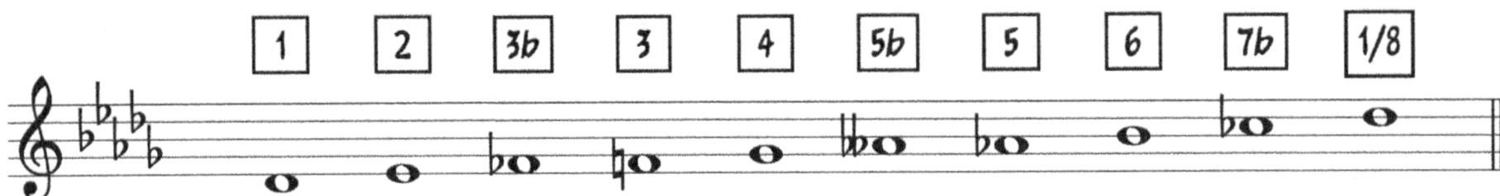

Shown As Named

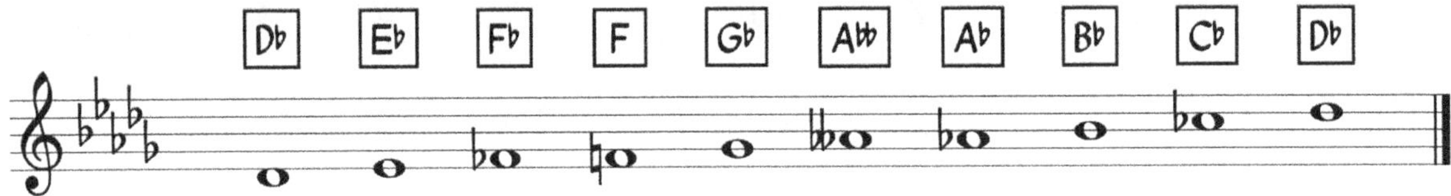

Fingering Suggestions   (Right-Hand)

1.   When not moving any higher.

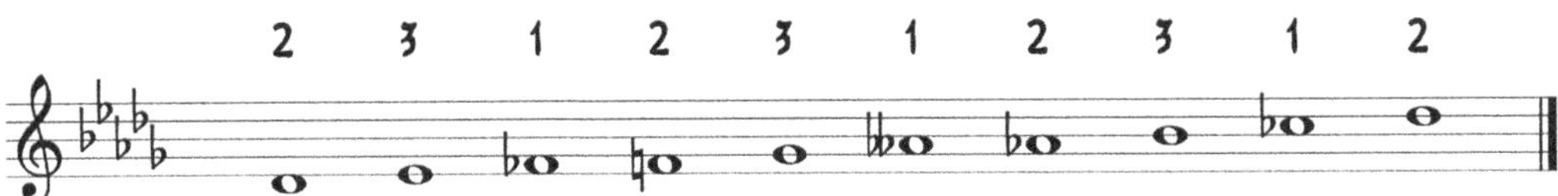

2.   When continuing on further up.

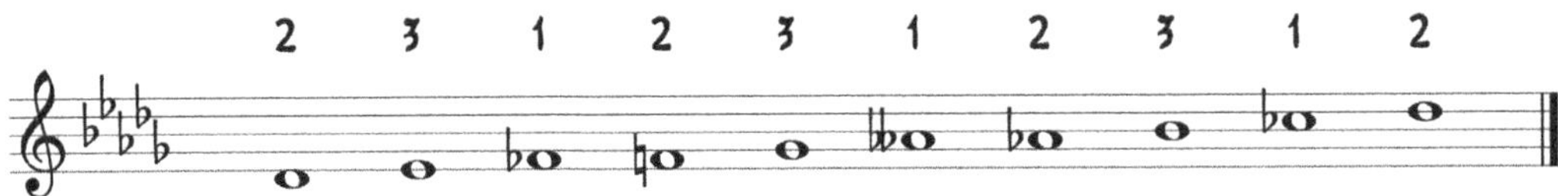

Due to the nature of this one the same fingering is probably best used regardless as to if it ends or continues further into a second octave.

D – Combined Scale

Practice over one octave to begin with, once comfortable with it, you can then extend the range to two and even three octaves.

Shown As Degrees

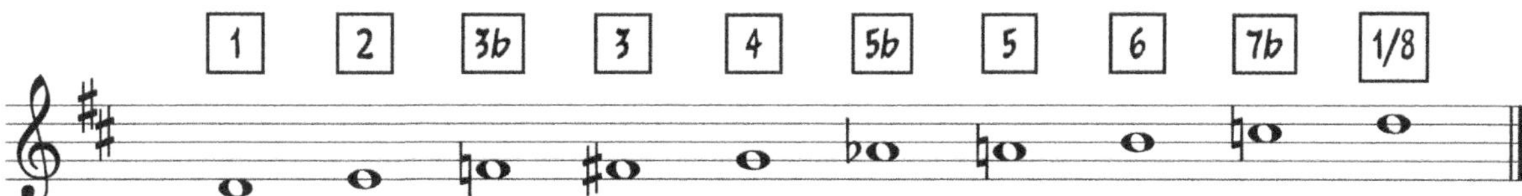

Shown As Named

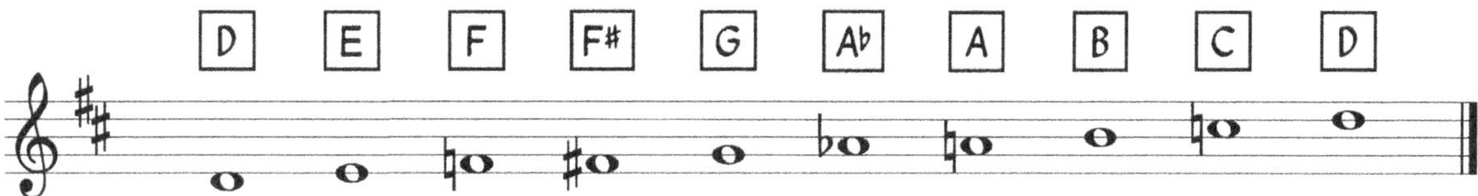

Fingering Suggestions (Right-Hand)

1.   When not moving any higher.

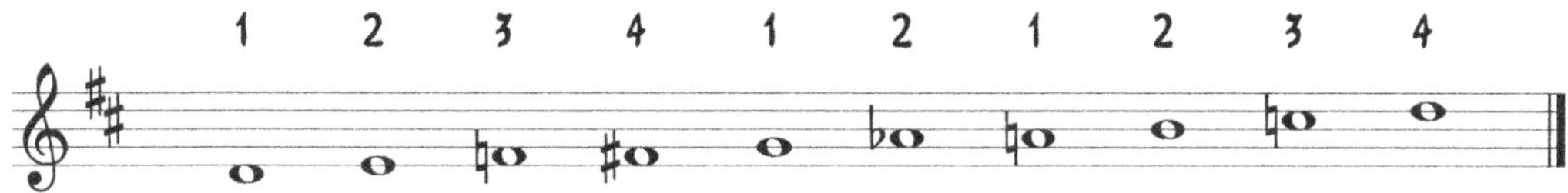

2.   When continuing on further up.

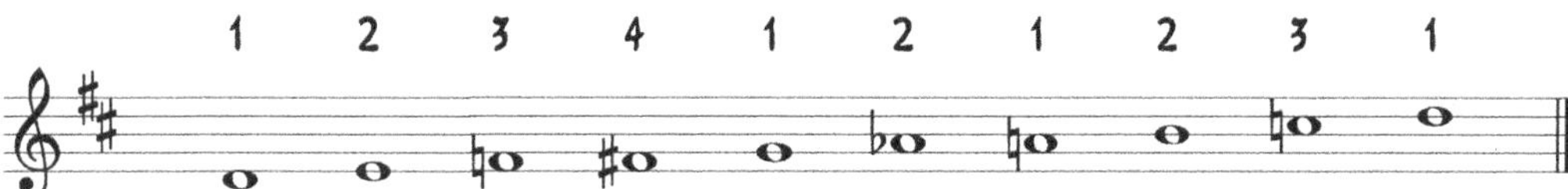

The thumb (1) is crossed over at the top onto the root note *if* the scale is to continue on up into another octave, otherwise finger (4) could be used at the top.

E♭ – Combined Scale

Practice over one octave to begin with, once comfortable with it, you can then extend the range to two and even three octaves.

Shown As Degrees

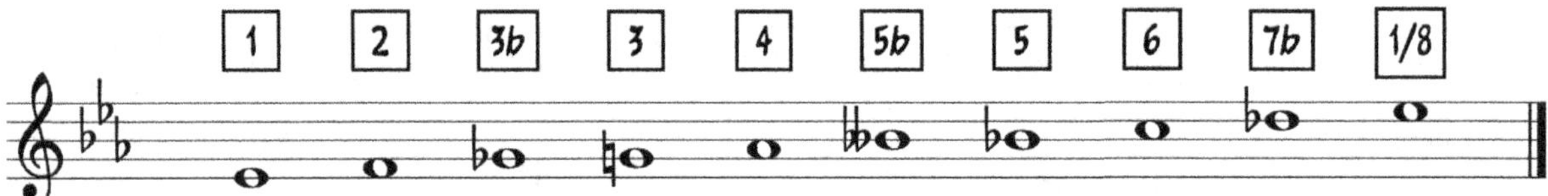

Shown As Named

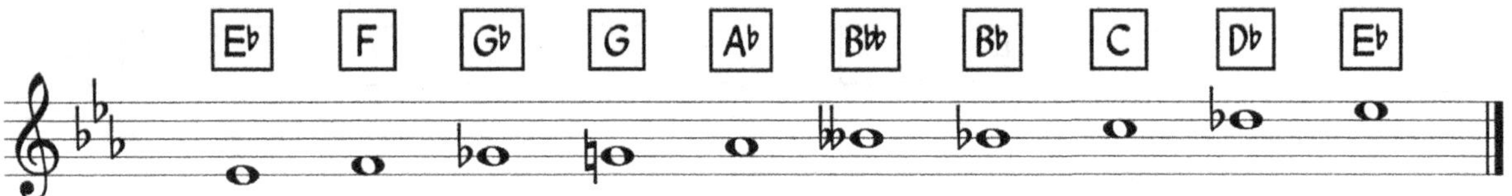

Fingering Suggestions   (Right-Hand)

1.   When not moving any higher.

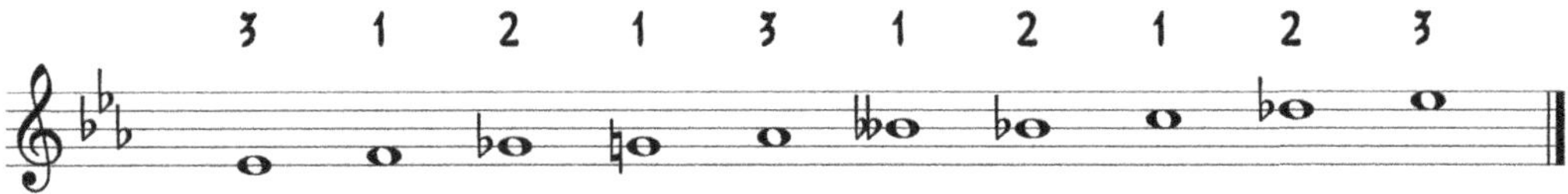

2.   When continuing on further up.

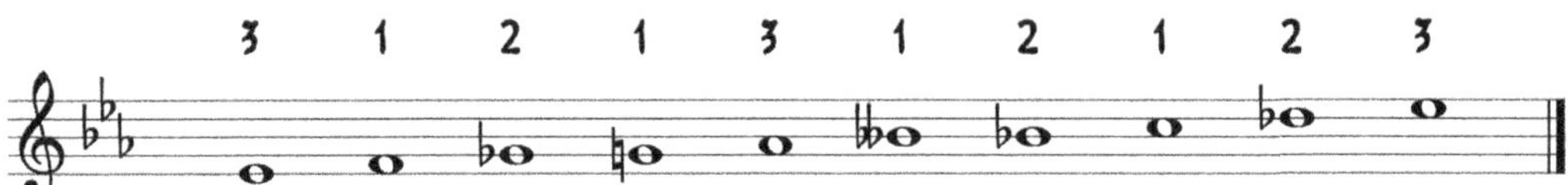

Due to the shape of the pattern it requires you to begin with finger (3). You can of course begin with (2) instead, but it's not possible to smoothly get that back onto the root note at the top if you wish to continue another octave higher.

E – Combined Scale

Practice over one octave to begin with, once comfortable with it, you can then extend the range to two and even three octaves.

Shown As Degrees

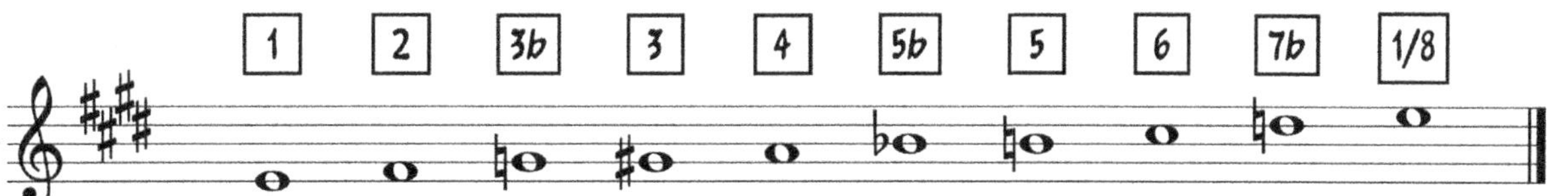

Shown As Named

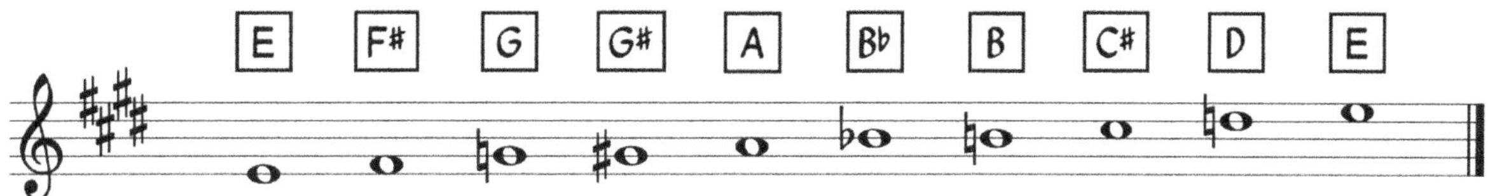

Fingering Suggestions   (Right-Hand)

1.   When not moving any higher.

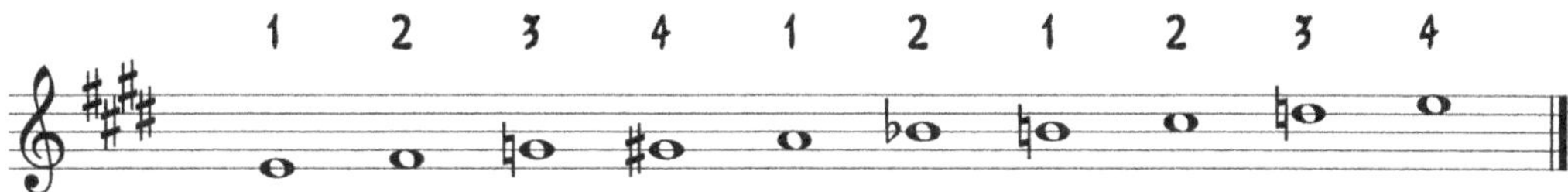

2.   When continuing on further up.

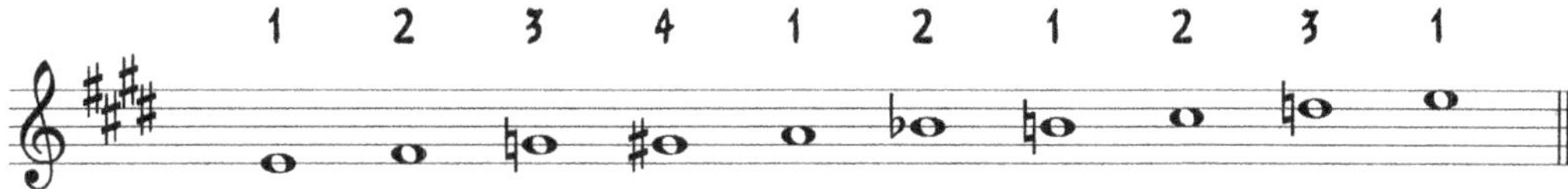

The thumb (1) is crossed over at the top to land back onto the root note *if* the scale is to continue up into another octave, otherwise finger (4) could be used at the top.

F – Combined Scale

Practice over one octave to begin with, once comfortable with it, you can then extend the range to two and even three octaves.

Shown As Degrees

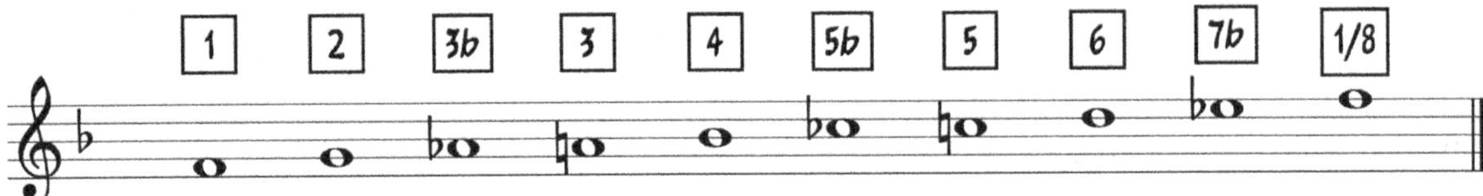

Shown As Named

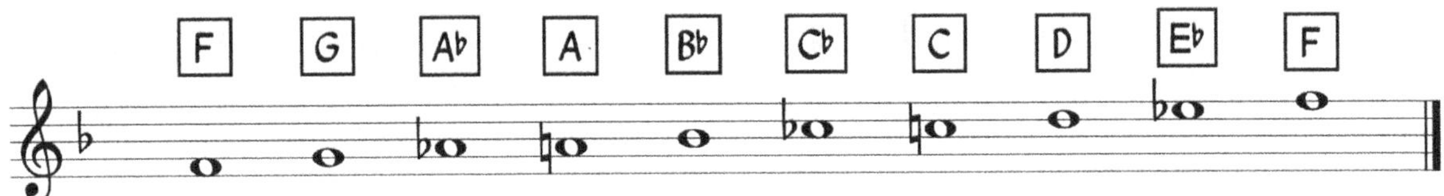

Fingering Suggestions (Right-Hand)

1. When not moving any higher.

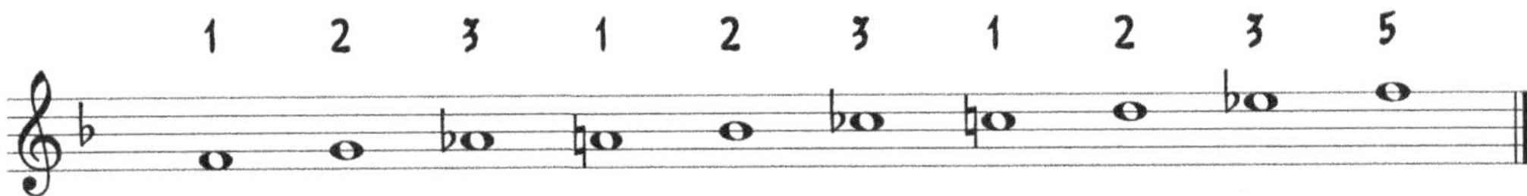

2. When continuing on further up.

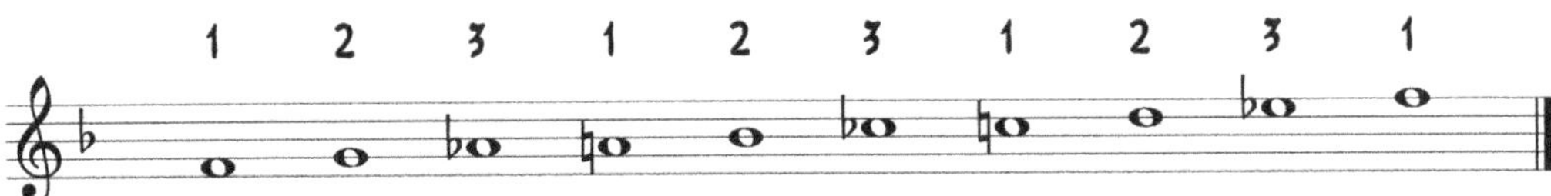

The thumb (1) is crossed over at the top to land back onto the root note *if* the scale is to continue up into another octave, otherwise finger (5) could be used at the top.

F♯ – Combined Scale

Practice over one octave to begin with, once comfortable with it, you can then extend the range to two and even three octaves.

Shown As Degrees

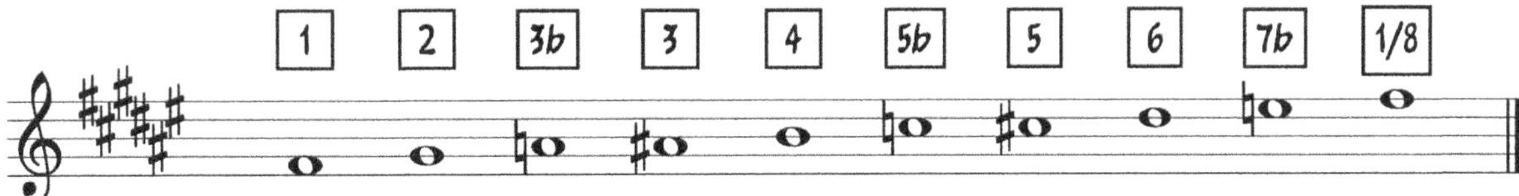

Shown As Named

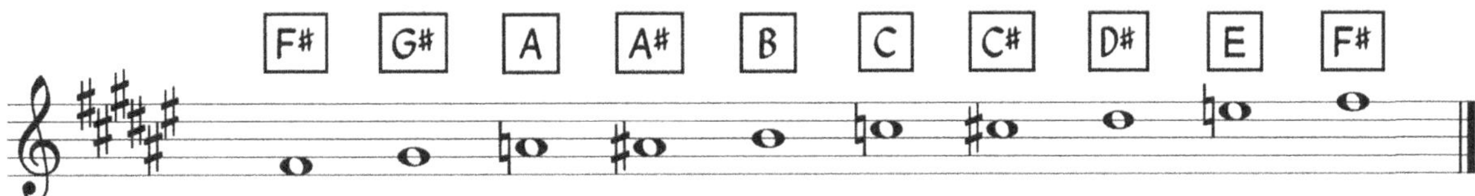

Fingering Suggestions   (Right-Hand)

1.   When not moving any higher.

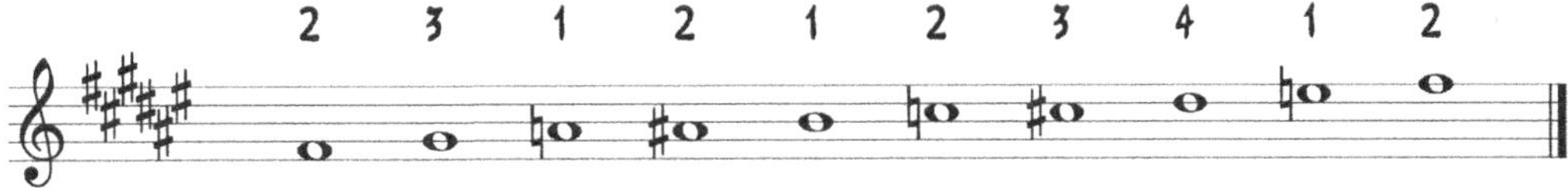

2.   When continuing on further up.

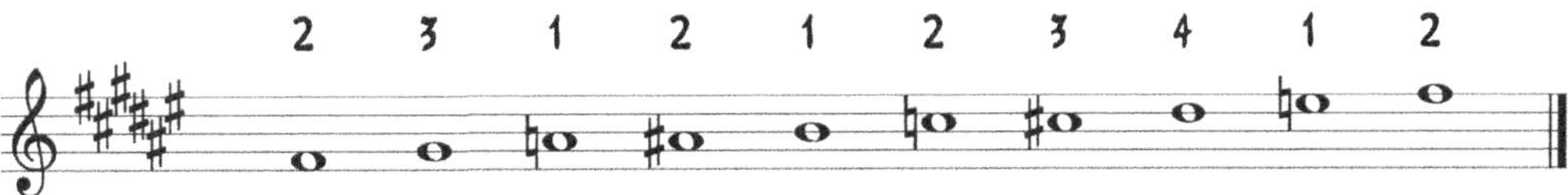

Due to the nature of this one the same fingering is probably best used regardless as to if it ends or continues further into a second octave.

G – Combined Scale

Practice over one octave to begin with, once comfortable with it, you can then extend the range to two and even three octaves.

Shown As Degrees

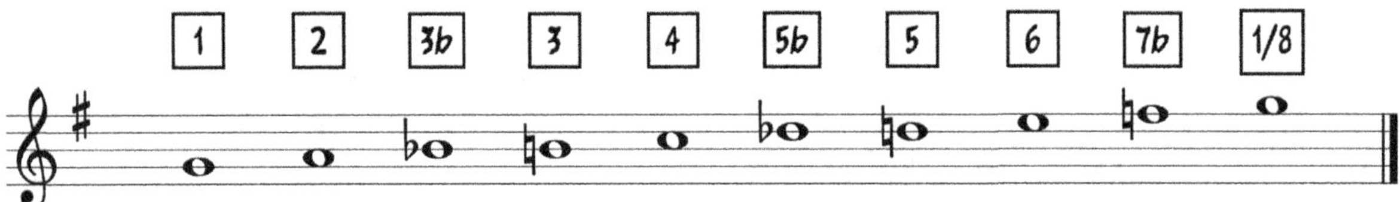

Shown As Named

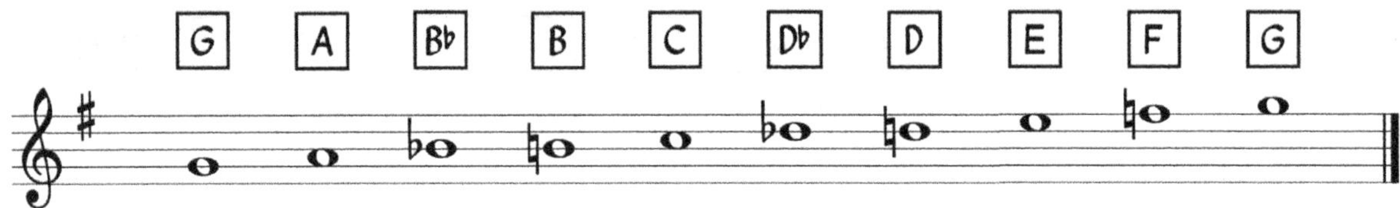

Fingering Suggestions   (Right-Hand)

1.   When not moving any higher.

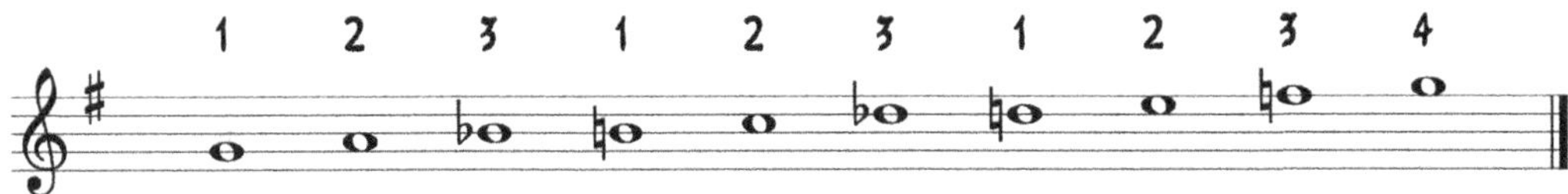

2.   When continuing on further up.

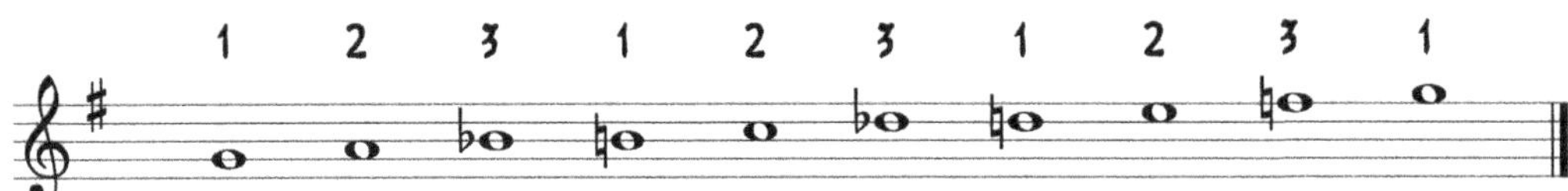

The thumb (1) is crossed over at the top to land back onto the root note *if* the scale is to continue up into another octave, otherwise finger (4) could be used at the top.

A♭ – Combined Scale

Practice over one octave to begin with, once comfortable with it, you can then extend the range to two and even three octaves.

Shown As Degrees

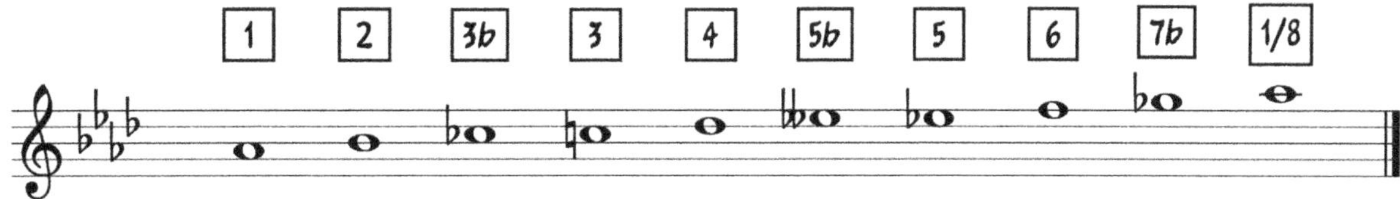

Shown As Named

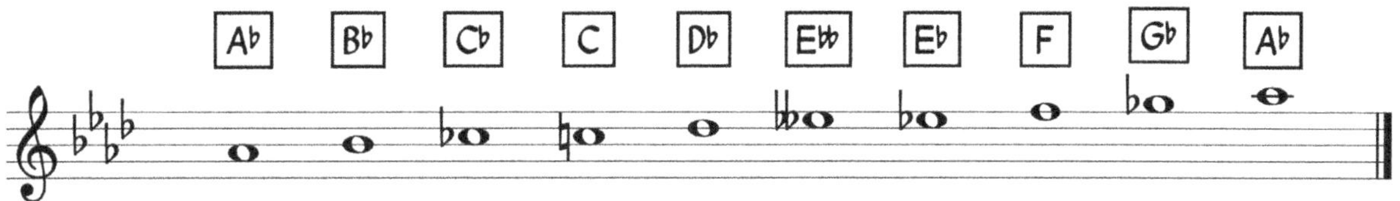

Fingering Suggestions (Right-Hand)

1. When not moving any higher.

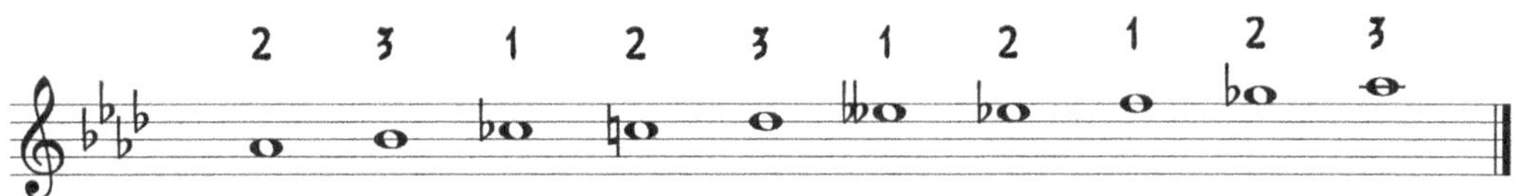

2. When continuing on further up.

Due to the nature of this one, it's difficult to finish with the starting finger (2), meaning that the next octave would begin with another finger, disrupting the pattern. Experiment with this and see what you can come up with.

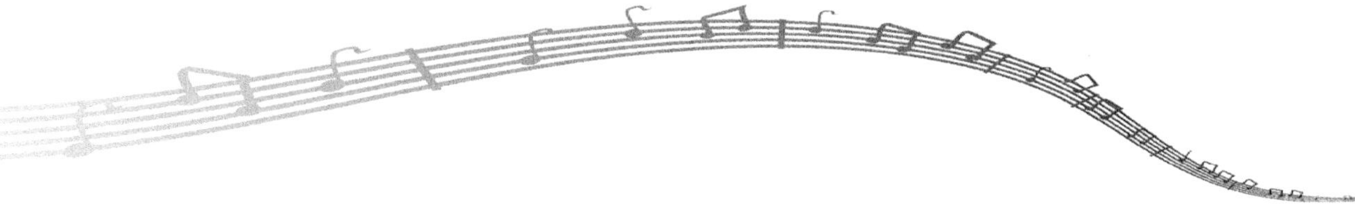

Practice Ideas

Practice Methods/Ideas

This section is about methods/ ideas of how to practice the scales in different ways in order to help with actual playing/improvising. Rather than simply learning the scales the typical way (up and down) which is limiting in its practical application, as it will become repetitive if there is no variation. Once you have got the basic scales memorised, and can efficiently run through them up and down, then it is time to look at other ways to practice them that will help in actual playing/improvising.

Important Notes

One Key Only

Due to size constraints of a book, or at least to keep things down to a publishable size, the following pages show examples in only one key (the key of 'C' for simplicity). This works well, as once a basic scale has been learnt then these ideas are simply about playing what's already known in a different order/pattern. So this is only applicable once that scale has been well memorised including knowing the degrees of that scale.

If you have any difficulties here then it's probably a case of going back and learning the basic scale a little better before moving on.

Right-Hand Bias

Also note that the practise examples given only include the right-hand, there is good reason for this. The music that the blues-scales are primarily used within are played in such a manner that the left-hand is normally doing its own thing, while it is the right-hand that will use the scales to play around/improvise with. This is especially true in traditional blues and boogie-woogie piano styles, which this book is primarily aimed at.

Now this doesn't mean you can't do this with the left-hand, but with time being a rare and valuable commodity, it isn't the best use of your time. It is traditional in classical music to practise scales using both hands, but this book is meant for a different market where the same rules don't quite apply. That said, it is totally up to the individual how they wish to learn, I will leave the choice entirety up to you.

Different Starting Points

When playing/improvising using blues-scales you won't necessarily begin a pattern/riff with the root note, so it's an idea to practice the scales by using different starting points (within the scale of course). The example shows the minor blues scale (key of C) starting from each note of the scale. Once you know a scale it's simple enough to then run through it using this method. It stops you being reliant on the root note to orient yourself within the scale and so help you drop into it from any point.

Root

Flat-Third

Fourth

Flat-Fifth

Fifth

Flat-Seventh

Alternating Starting Points

Alternatively, run up the scale (root to root) and then run down the scale but from a starting point a degree of the scale higher. So minor-blues, up from the root and down from the flat-third, up from the fourth and down from the flat-fifth and so on and so on.

Minor-Blues

Root And Flat-Third

Fourth And Flat-Fifth

Fifth And Flat-Seventh

Major Blues

Root And Second

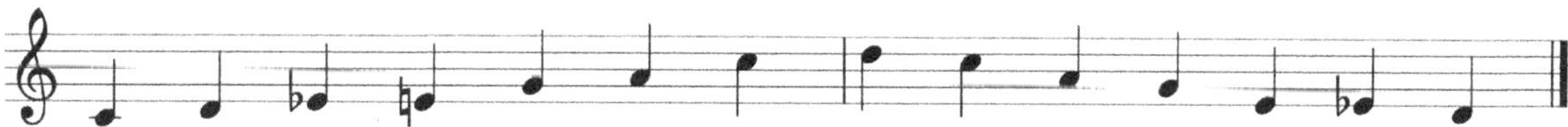

Flat-Third And Third

Fifth And Sixth

Using Octaves

It's quite common practice to play using octaves at times, so it's a good idea to practice playing octaves using the blues-scales. Once these are well practised and internalised it enables you to move up or down using the scales in octaves with little thought and remaining accurate.

A few different ways to go about this are shown below. Starting by moving up and down the scale, first over one octave and then two. Then you might what to practice playing them with a triplet timing (being a common aspect of blues based music) with two options shown below. The last example (playing all three triplets) is quite physical and will certainly give you a work-out.

1.   One Octave Up And Down

2.   Two Octaves Up And Down

3.   Triplet Timing. 1

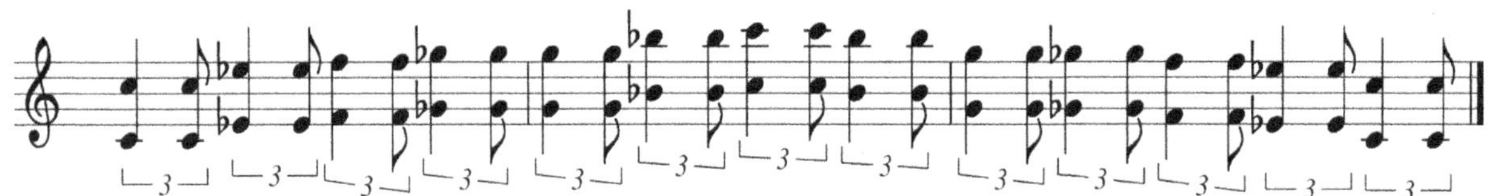

4.   Triplet Timing. 2

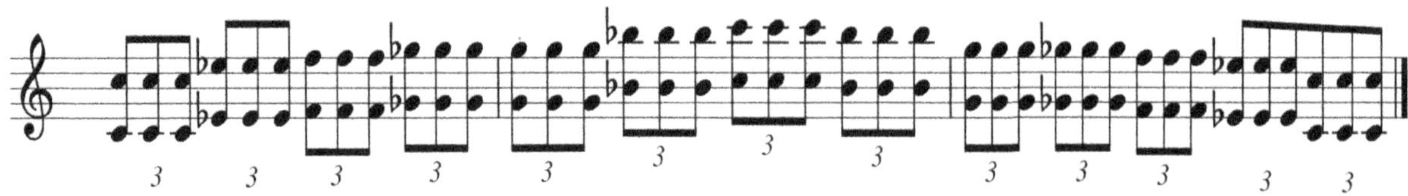

Three Note Groupings (Minor)

Three Note Grouping No.1

Moving up through the scale using just two different notes of the scale per three note grouping. The starting note of each grouping shifts up one note (within the scale) with each successive grouping.

Moving Up Two Octaves

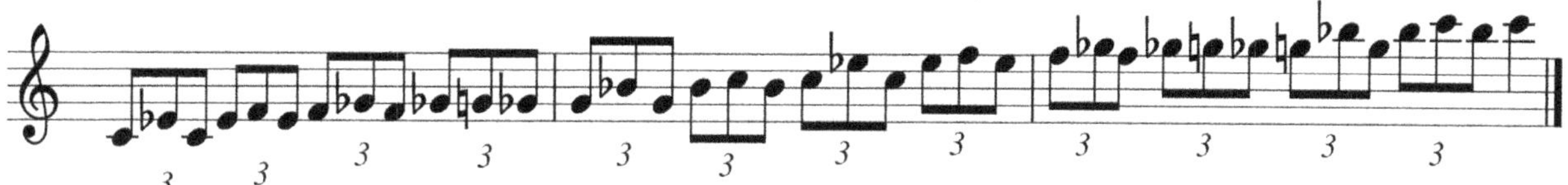

Moving Down Two Octaves

Degrees Of Scale In Order Used   (Upwards)

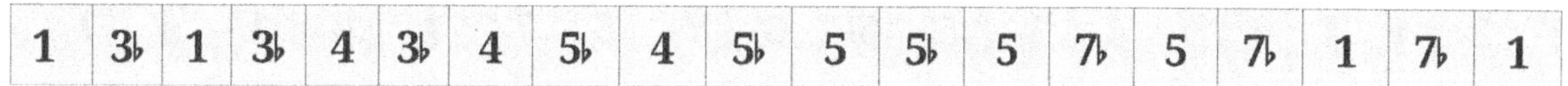

Degrees Of Scale In Order Used   (Downwards)

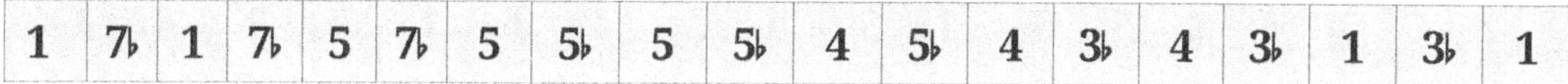

Three Note Groupings (Minor)

Three Note Grouping No.2

Moving up through the scale using three notes of the scale per three note grouping. The starting point shifts up one note (within the scale) with each successive grouping.

Moving Up Two Octaves

Moving Down Two Octaves

Degrees Of Scale In Order Used   (Upwards)

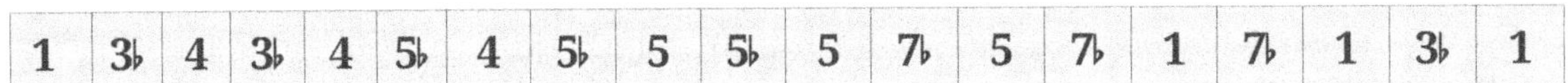

Degrees Of Scale In Order Used   (Downwards)

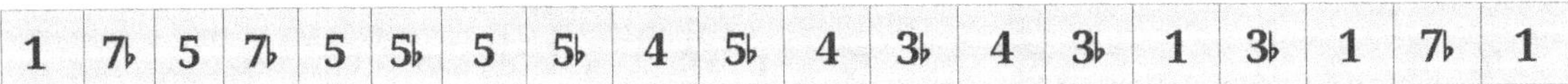

Three Note Groupings (Minor)

Three Note Grouping No.3

Moving up through the scale using three notes of the scale per three note grouping. This time the pattern moves up and down, alternating with each three note group. Each successive three note grouping starts one note higher (within the scale) than the previous one ended.

Moving Up Two Octaves

Moving Down Two Octaves

Degrees Of Scale In Order Used   (Upwards)

Degrees Of Scale In Order Used   (Downwards)

Three Note Groupings (Major)

Three Note Grouping No.1

Moving through the scale using two notes of the scale per three note grouping. The starting point of each grouping shifts up one note (within the scale) with each successive grouping.

Moving Up Two Octaves

Moving Down Two Octaves

Degrees Of Scale In Order Used   (Upwards)

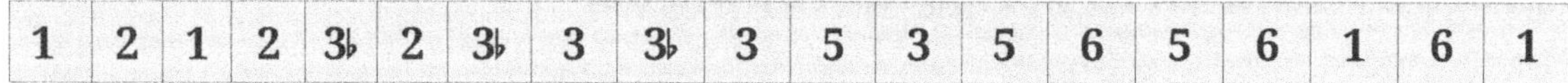

Degrees Of Scale In Order Used   (Downwards)

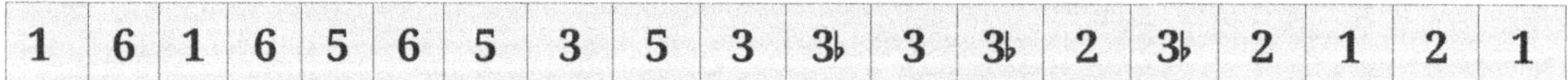

Three Note Groupings (Major)

Three Note Grouping No.2

Moving through the scale using three notes of the scale per three note grouping. Again the starting point shifts up one note (within the scale) with each successive grouping.

Moving Up Two Octaves

Moving Down Two Octaves

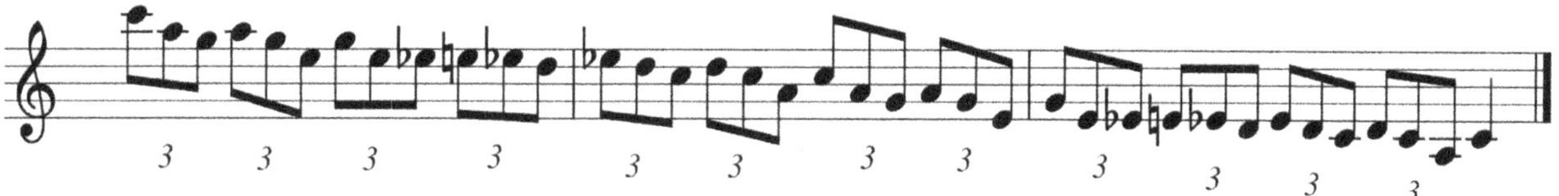

Degrees Of Scale In Order Used   (Upwards)

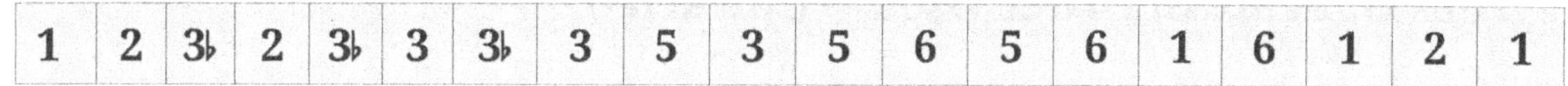

Degrees Of Scale In Order Used   (Downwards)

Three Note Groupings (Major)

Three Note Grouping No.3

Moving through the scale using three notes of the scale per three note grouping. This time the pattern moves up and down, alternating with each three note grouping. Each successive three note grouping starts one note higher (within the scale) than where the previous one ended.

Moving Up Two Octaves

Moving Down Two Octaves

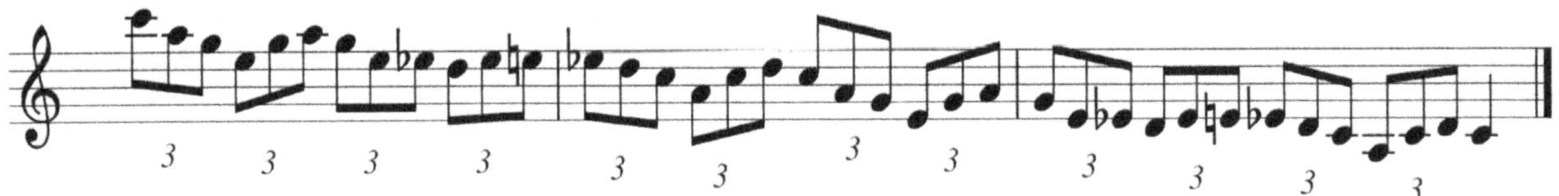

Degrees Of Scale In Order Used   (Upwards)

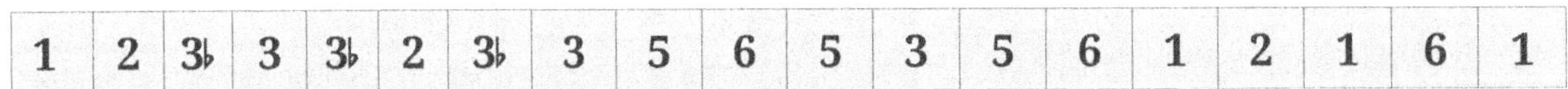

Degrees Of Scale In Order Used   (Downwards)

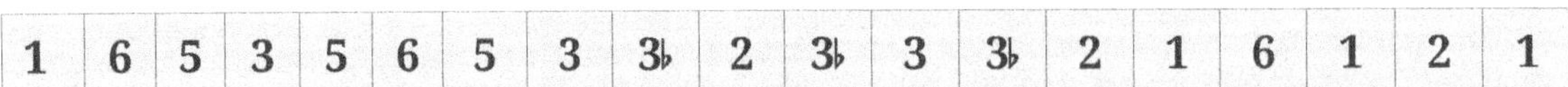

Four Note Groupings (Minor)

Four Note Grouping

Moving through the scale using four notes of the scale per four note grouping. The starting point shifts up one note (within the scale) with each successive grouping.

Moving Up Two Octaves

Moving Down Two Octaves

Degrees Of Scale In Order Used   (Upwards)

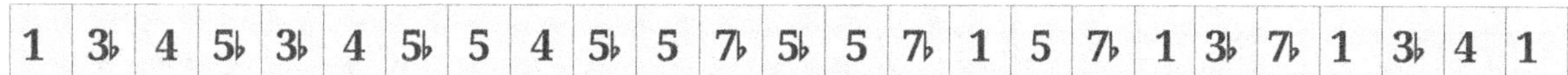

Degrees Of Scale In Order Used   (Downwards)

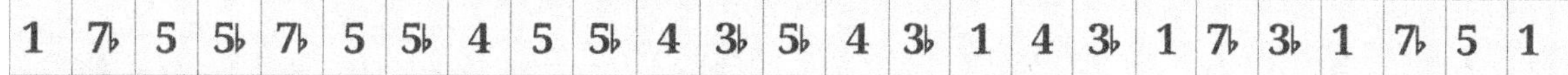

Four Note Groupings (Major)

Four Note Grouping

Moving through the scale using four notes of the scale per four note grouping. The starting point shifts up one note (within the scale) with each successive grouping.

Moving Up Two Octaves

Moving Down Two Octaves

Degrees Of Scale In Order Used   (Upwards)

Degrees Of Scale In Order Used   (Downwards)

Blues Scale Runs

Five And Five

Here we are moving down through the scale (minor) using five note groupings. Play through the first five notes of the scale but then stop and move back up two places (within the scale) and move down again through five notes of the scale. Repeat over and over.

Degrees Of Scale In Order Used

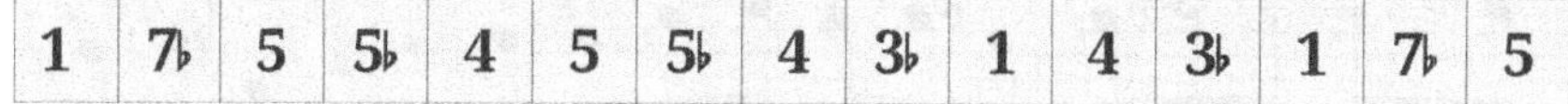

1	7♭	5	5♭	4	5	5♭	4	3♭	1	4	3♭	1	7♭	5

Six And Six (Alternative)

This is the same basic idea but with an additional note added at the end of the previous five note grouping

Degrees Of Scale In Order Used

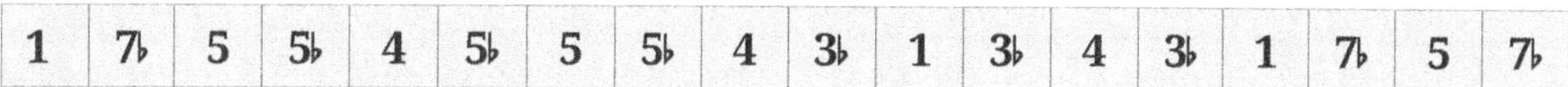

1	7♭	5	5♭	4	5♭	5	5♭	4	3♭	1	3♭	4	3♭	1	7♭	5	7♭

Root And Flat-Fifth (No.1)

Here we are moving down through the minor scale, beginning on the root note and moving down to the root an octave below. From here, jump up to the flat-fifth and continue down through the scale to the fifth an octave below before stepping back up to the seventh.

This pattern can be repeated moving down again and again, below shows the pattern repeating three times.

Three Times Down

Degrees Of Scale In Order Used

1	7♭	5	5♭	4	3♭	1	5♭	4	3♭	1	7♭	5	7♭

Root And Flat-Fifth (No.2)

Move down through the scale (minor) beginning on the root note and moving down to the root an octave below, from here move back up through the scale to the flat-fifth and then back down to end on the flat-seventh.

This pattern can be repeated moving down again and again, below shows the pattern repeating three times.

Three Times Down

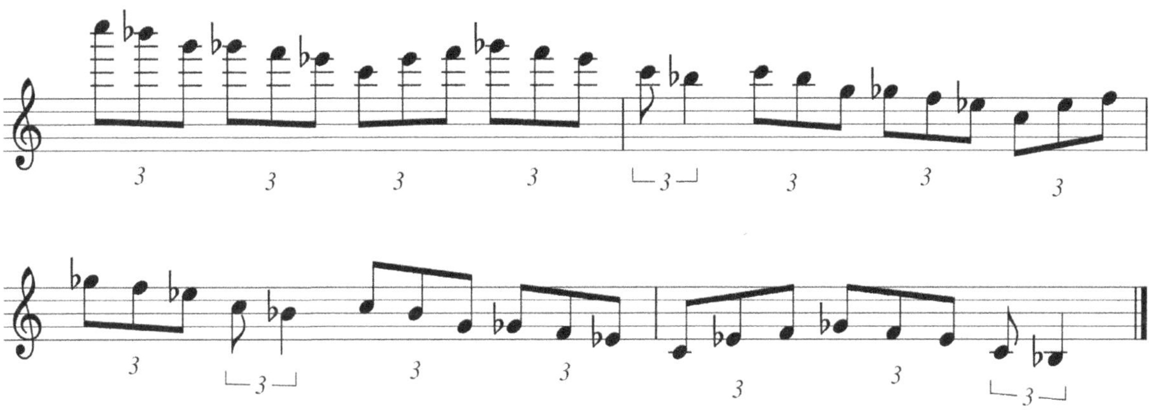

Degrees Of Scale In Order Used

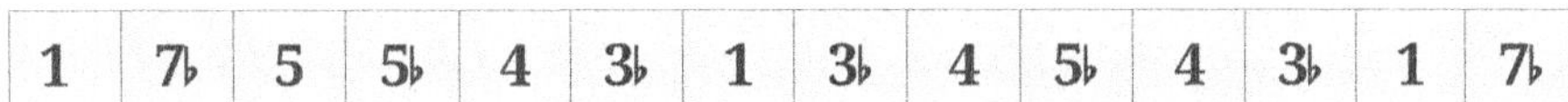

Root And Flat-Fifth (No.3)

Moving down through the minor scale, begin on the root note and move down to the root an octave below. From here, jump up to the flat-fifth and then down to the root (done twice) followed by the flat-seventh and fifth and flat-seventh.

This pattern can be repeated moving down again and again, below shows the pattern repeating twice.

Two Times Run

Degrees Of Scale In Order Used

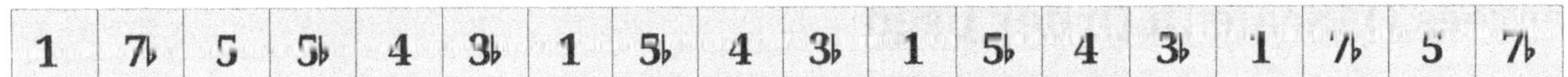

1	7♭	5	5♭	4	3♭	1	5♭	4	3♭	1	5♭	4	3♭	1	7♭	5	7♭

Root And Fourth (Down)

Moving down through the scale (minor) begin on the root note and move down to the root an octave below, from here jump up to the fourth and continue down through the scale to the fourth an octave below.

This pattern can be repeated moving down again and again, here shown running down for four octaves, root to root note.

Four Octave Run

Degrees Of Scale In Order Used

1	7♭	5	5♭	4	3♭	1	4	3♭	1	7♭	5	5♭	4

Root And Fourth (Up)

Here we are moving up through the minor scale, beginning on the root note and moving up to the seventh. From here, jump down to the fourth and then continue up through the scale to the root, from here it can be repeated.

This pattern can be repeated moving up again and again, here shown running up four octaves, root to root.

Four Octave Run

Degrees Of Scale In Order Used

1	3♭	4	5♭	5	7♭	4	5♭	5	7♭	1

Root And Sixth (Up)

Move up through the scale (major) going from root to root, from there step back to the sixth and then continue on through the scale to the root.

This pattern can be repeated moving up again, here shown running up the pattern twice.

Double Run

Degrees Of Scale In Order Used

Alternating Pattern (Minor)

Here we are moving up through the minor scale using an alternating pattern. This alternates between the base note (root) and each degree of the scale until it reaches the seventh, here the base note is changed to the fifth for two beats before becoming the root note once again.

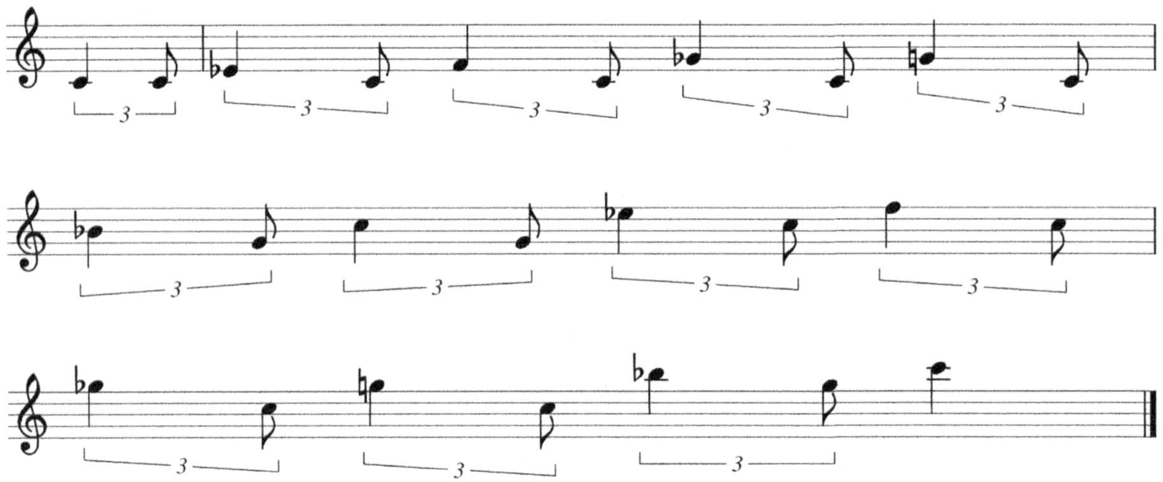

Longer Run

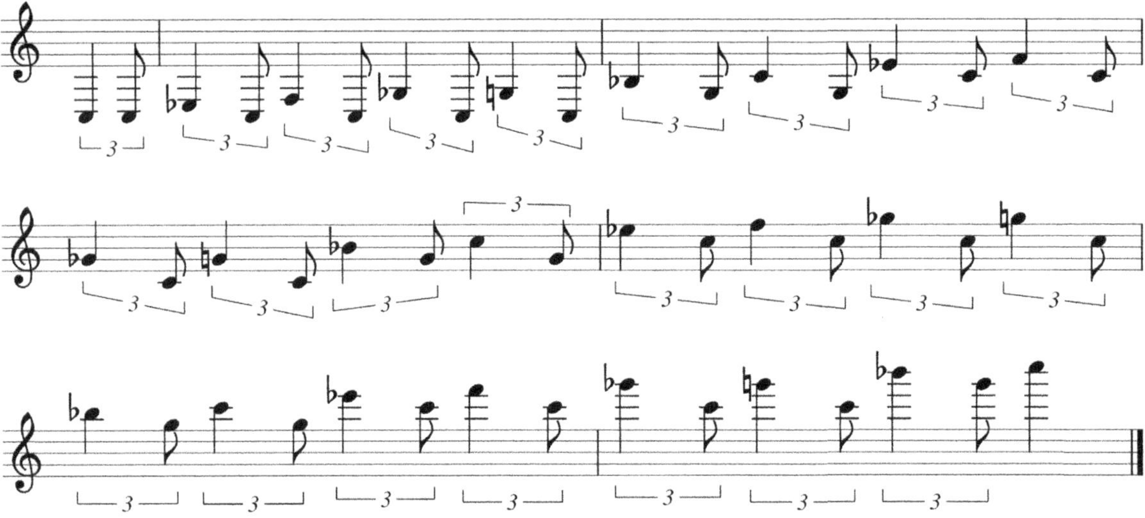

Degrees Of Scale In Order Used

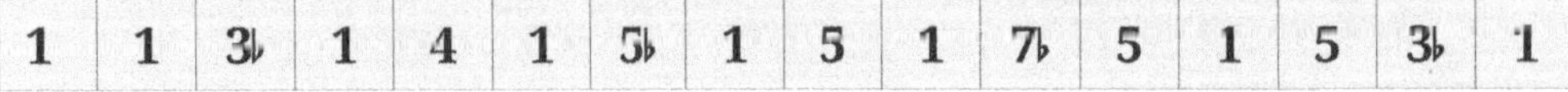

Alternating Pattern (Major)

Here we are moving up through the major scale using an alternating pattern. This alternates between the base note (root) and each degree of the scale until it reaches the fifth, here the base note is changes to the third, fifth, and sixth before becoming the root note once again.

Longer Run

Degrees Of Scale In Order Used

1	1	3♭	1	4	1	5♭	1	5	1	7♭	5	1	5	3♭	1

Practice Over Left-Hand

After you have spent some time with the scales on their own it can be a good idea to then practice them while playing with the left-hand at the same time. Being that these are 'blues-scales' this book is focused towards blues and boogie-woogie piano, as such the following examples will be based on such styles. Here are just a few examples to push you in the right direction as there are so many variations that you could come up with to help you practice.

Examples are in the key 'C' but obviously use the same idea for any key that you are practicing. Also remember that you can extend the range that you play over, from one or two octaves to three or four if you desire. The longer you make it the harder it becomes to keep it flowing.

Example. 1

The simplest form is to play a scale up and down over one octave whilst playing a boogie-woogie style bass with the left-hand.

Example. 2

Here the timing of the right-hand has changed which then requires three bars to move up and down through a minor-blues scale over two octaves.

Example. 3

Using one of the alternating patterns that move up through the scale using a three note grouping as it ascends.

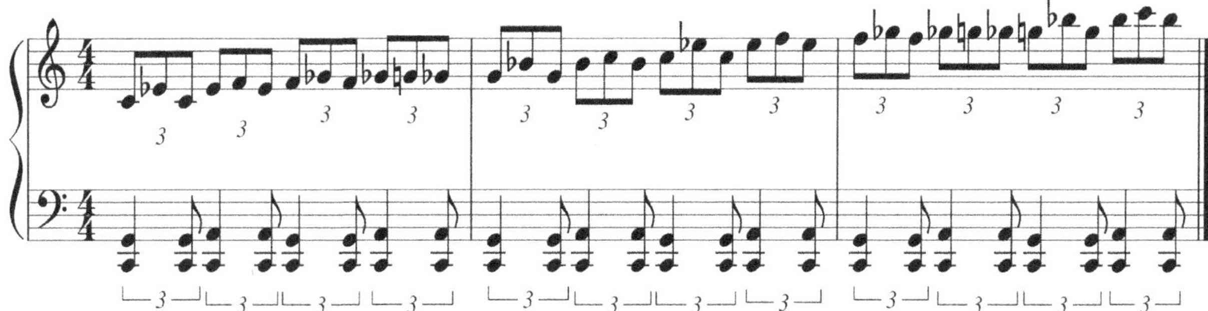

Example. 4

This uses one of the descending patterns that jumps up to the flat-fifth mid-way.

Example. 5

Playing the scales using octaves over the left-hand.

Example. 6

As an alternative you could try playing the scale in octaves, here shown as an alternating pattern between the left and right hands, with the left-hand following the right.

FURTHER PRACTICE IDEAS

You can take the same basic idea shown in the examples and create new ways to practice your chosen scale (be it minor or major blues) using any left-hand pattern of your choice (assuming that it fits of course). Just take any left-hand pattern that you know and try playing the scales over the top in various incarnations and do the same thing in all the keys that are relevant to you, it's as simple as that. Practicing the scales over the left-hand will help when it comes to incorporating them into your actual playing, rather than just playing the scales alone, as that isn't quite as musical.

Tyler music.co.uk

Website And Online Book-Shop
For further piano books (including spiral bound editions)
sheet music and information on blues
and boogie woogie music
visit the website at…

www.tylermusic.co.uk

Follow us on Facebook for updates
and information on new releases.

Also Available

Improvising Boogie-Woogie Vol. One

Learn to play boogie-woogie like the best of them. If you want to play boogie like Albert Ammons, Axel Zwingenberger or Jools Holland then this is the series for you. The first volume in a series of books to teach boogie-woogie piano, from the basics to more advanced techniques and everything in-between, this will give you the help and material you need.

Improvising Boogie-Woogie Vol. Two

The ultimate guide to playing boogie-woogie continues with volume-two, adding more left-hand patterns and right-hand riffs, including aspects like the walking-bass pattern, a little stride, rolling chords, using tenths and more complex rhythmic ideas.

Improvising Boogie-Woogie Vol. Three

The ultimate guide to playing boogie-woogie continues with volume-three, adding even more left-hand patterns and right-hand riffs to the series. Looking at the use of thirds and sixths, the use of scaler other chord progressions how such riffs are created and how to begin to create your own.

Improvising Boogie-Woogie: The Complete Edition

All three volumes in one edition. Available as perfect bound and spiral bound (spiral available through the website only). Learn to play boogie-woogie like the best of them. If you want to play boogie like Albert Ammons, Axel Zwingenberger or Jools Holland then this is the series for you. From the basics to more advanced techniques and everything in-between.

Easy New-Orleans   For Beginners

Learn to play that unique style of blues piano from New Orleans, the style of Dr John, Professor Longhair and James Booker to name but a few. Covering everything from chord progressions and left-hand bass patterns and introducing the all important New-Orleans rhythm.

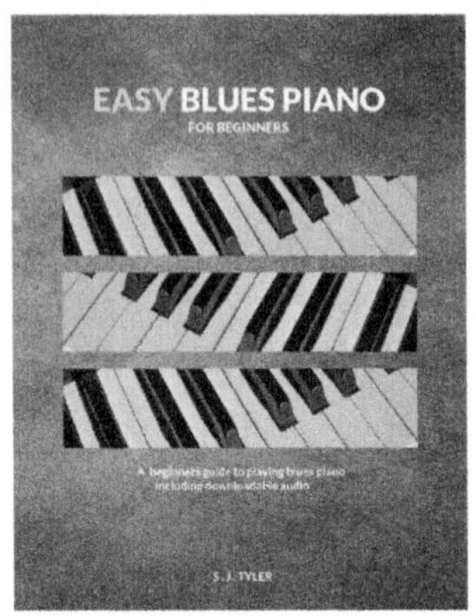

Easy Blues Piano   For Beginners

Learn to play the blues with this beginners guide for the piano. It covers the very basics of the blues, introducing the various elements that create the twelve-bar blues sound. It starts off easy, so even a relative beginner can dive in, and gradually introduces new ideas. With downloadable audio,why not start learning blues today.

Easy Rock 'N' Roll   For Beginners

Easy rock 'n' roll is for the beginner taking their first steps into the timeless sound of rock 'n' roll piano. Covering the basics with easy to understand clear explanations on how to play in the style of the likes of Jerry Lee Lewis and Little Richard. It includes example pieces throughout that start off easy and gradually increase in difficulty, while adding extra elements along the way. With downloadable audio

The Complete Blues Piano

The complete blues piano is a comprehensive guide to playing and improvising blues piano. It covers the fundamental principles of the blues and includes in-depth theory and techniques, along with example blues pieces to learn/study with downloadable audio. Ranging from fast boogie-type blues to slow blues, Chicago through to New Orleans, beginners to intermediate, this has it covered.

Easy Boogie-Woogie Vol.2

This second volume of Easy Boogie-Woogie follows on from the first one, taking the beginning boogie player a step further again. New ideas and concepts are introduced along with many examples and explanations throughout. Bigger and better than ever. With downloadable audio to help you along, it's the perfect way to continue your boogie-woogie journey.

The Essential Elements Of Blues Piano Volume One Walking-Bass Techniques

Learn to play the walking-bass for blues piano with the first in a series that concentrates on specific aspects of blues piano. Concentrating on the left-hand, it looks at what the walking-bass is, how it is created and various ways to which you can employ it in a blues environment.

The Essential Elements Of Blues Piano Volume Two Stride Piano Techniques

Learn to play blues piano using the left-hand stride style. The second in a series that concentrates on a specific aspect of blues piano. Concentrating on the left-hand, it looks at what stride is and how it is created and various ways to which you can employ it in a blues environment.

The Essential Elements Of Blues Piano Volume Three Right-Hand Comping Techniques

Learn to play blues piano with the third in a series that concentrates on specific aspects of blues piano. Concentrating on the right-hand, and the important aspect of comping, which is the more rhythmic side of blues with an emphasis on the important use of chords and repetitive patterns/riffs that form the backbone of the music.

Made in the USA
Monee, IL
07 July 2026

56644838R00050